The Word Whiz's Guide to Florida Middle School Vocabulary

By Chris Kensler

A Paper Airplane Project

Simon & Schuster
New York ● London ● Sydney ● Singapore ● Toronto

Kaplan Publishing
Published by Simon & Schuster, Inc.
1230 Avenue of the Americas
New York, NY 10020

For bulk sales to schools, colleges, and universities, please contact: Order Department,
Simon & Schuster, 100 Front Street, Riverside, NJ 08075. Phone: 1-800-223-2336. Fax:
1-800-943-9831.

Kaplan® is a registered trademark of Kaplan, Inc.

Cover Design: Cheung Tai
Interior Page Design and Production: Paper Airplane Projects

Manufactured in the United States of America

September 2001

10 9 8 7 6 5 4 3 2 1

Library of Congress Cataloging-in-Publication Data

ISBN 0-7432-1107-3

All of the practice questions in this book were created by the authors to illustrate question types. They are not actual test questions.

Table of Contents

About the Author

Chris Kensler grew up in Indiana and attended Indiana University, where he majored in English. He has edited test prep publications, worked as feature writer/reporter for a daytime drama publication, and written a few books, including *Study Smart Junior*, which received the Parents' Choice Award. Currently, he is the editor of an art magazine, is married to the lovely woman who designed this book, and has some cool cats and a dog named Joe.

Mort Lauderdale is a figment of his imagination.

Acknowledgments

The author would like to thank Maureen McMahon, Lori DeGeorge, and Beth Grupper for their help in shaping and editing the manuscript, and Chris Dreyer for copyediting this book.

The publisher wishes to thank Ryan Blanchette for his contributions to this book.

Introduction

Hi. My name is Mort. Mort Lauderdale. As
you can probably tell from my name, I'm from Fort Lauderdale, Florida. I'm going to help you with your vocabulary.

I'm in the eighth grade. At my school I'm famous for two things—my long drives and my vocabulary. I perfected my golf swing last summer by going to the range for two hours every day. Now my drives go up to 200 yards—not bad for an eighth grader. And I don't like to brag, but my play around the greens is probably better than Phil Mickelson's.

I perfected my vocabulary by practicing, too. By reading books, writing essays and stories, and by just generally paying attention to words. It turned me into a Word Whiz. Now I'm going to turn you into one.

If you're having trouble on tests, one reason might be because you are having trouble understanding the words. Of course, the first and most likely reason you blank or panic or freak out on tests is that instead of studying, you keep watching your new *Chicken Run* DVD. Still, sometimes things don't go so well even when you do study. That's the worst. You're like—I studied all night and I still got a D! What's up with that?

Sometimes it's because you just aren't comfortable with the words on the test. For example, say you are taking a math test and one of the questions asks you to find the "perimeter of a rectangle." It's not hard to do—you just add up all the sides. But if you space out on what the word "perimeter" means, you're in trouble. Your brain freezes. Does it have something to do with periscopes? Or maybe something to do with meters? The next thing you know, you have a picture of a submarine doing the 40-meter dash in your head.

Believe me, I've been there. It's no fun. But it doesn't have to be that way.

Word Whiz Is Here to Help

Believe it or not, you probably already know more than 10,000 words total. It just happens. The older you get, the more words get added to your vocabulary. But let's not talk about the words you already know; let's focus on the words you need to know. The more than 600 words in this book are the most important ones to know for middle school homework, tests, and the FCAT (Florida Comprehensive Assessment Test). I call them WhizWords. If you know these WhizWords backward and forward, you will be in good shape at school, and you will no doubt become rich and successful when you grow up.

I'm going to review these WhizWords for you by relating them to things you're probably interested in, like TV, movies, sports, music, celebrities, and the stuff kids like us like to do when we're NOT in school. All these things can help you learn these crucial words.

5

I'm also going to explain them to you in words you already know. The problem with a lot of dictionaries is the words they use in the definition are harder than the word they are defining! Or they just repeat the word. Here's an example—the definition of "impartial" from a popular dictionary (I won't name names):

impartial—*adj.* not partial; unprejudiced.

Gee, thanks a lot! Believe me, if I knew what "partial" meant, I could probably figure out impartial. And "unprejudiced?" How many syllables is that? Eleven? Geez. And of course they don't give a sample sentence. Now here's my definition:

impartial—*adj.* fair. Judges and juries are supposed to be <u>impartial</u>. That means they just go by the facts. Like Judge Judy on TV —she is an <u>impartial</u> judge who listens to all the facts, then she reams the person who is guilty.

Better, right? I'm also only going to give you the one or two meanings that you are most likely to see on a test or in class. Some words have tons of different meanings, and regular dictionaries have to list them all. But in my book, I am just going to focus on the meanings that apply to your tests, classroom reading, and homework.

How to Use This Book

Most dictionaries just list all words in alphabetical order. That's a good idea, of course. But I have gone one step further. My WhizWords are in alphabetical order, but I have also divided them into six categories:

Language Arts　　　　**Science**
Social Studies　　　　**Test Instructions**
Math　　　　　　　　**All-Purpose Words**

This way, you can focus on the subjects where you want to improve your vocabulary. I've also included a list of words that you'll probably come across when you're taking the FCAT or other tests, and another list of general words that you'll find useful in all your classes.

Now, each of these chapters has two parts—the vocabulary list, plus some practice exercises. The exercises will help you remember important words that are related to each other. Off to the side of the exercises, you'll see a bunch of icons. These tell you what resources you'll use for the exercise—things like TV, newspapers, and the Internet. These are the icons:

Life　　　School　　　Movie　　　Sports　　　Magazine

History　Imagination　News　　Internet　Television

These exercises are like dessert. The main course of the book is my WhizWord lists. They give you easy-to-understand definitions and sample sentences like the one I gave you for "impartial." You'll also find all this extra cool stuff:

 My helpful hints on how to learn words and ace tests.

 Really short quizzes to help cement the words in your brain.

 Good stuff to know that is related to a WhizWord.

DOUBLE MEANING WhizWords that can mean two different things.

 Words that mean the same thing as a WhizWord.

 Words that mean the opposite of a WhizWord.

 An important word related to a WhizWord.

 How WhizWords are likely to appear on the FCAT.

Okay then. I think I'm done explaining. Have fun, and remember, if you learn all these words, your vocabulary will be really, really good and you should do better on your tests. It's a better way to live. Peace.

Mort Lauderdale

Chapter 1

Language Arts

Use an adjective or adverb to describe each of these words:
school
shopping
tests
green
sports
chewy

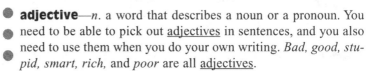

adjective—*n.* a word that describes a noun or a pronoun. You need to be able to pick out <u>adjectives</u> in sentences, and you also need to use them when you do your own writing. *Bad, good, stupid, smart, rich,* and *poor* are all <u>adjectives</u>.

adverb—*n.* a word that describes a verb, an adjective, or another adverb. What I just said for adjectives goes for <u>adverbs</u>. You can remember what words an <u>adverb</u> modifies because the parts of speech it modifies are part of its name: ad- (adjectives, adverbs) and -<u>verb</u> (verbs). *Very, really, not, incredibly, amazingly,* and *obviously* are all <u>adverbs</u>.

alliteration—*n.* the appearance of two or more words with the same initial sound in a sentence or phrase. Example: Slothy S. Slothster sank slowly into the sofa, sighing.

analogous—*adj.* alike; the same. For me, hitting a golf ball is <u>analogous</u> to eating a pack of Skittles. I love them both the same amount.

analogy—*n.* a comparison between two things made in order to explain or clarify an idea. *Example*: During the post-presidential-election controversy in 2000, Bush and Gore supporters disagreed about practically everything. Oil and water do not mix.

analyze—*v.* to study closely. My dad <u>analyzed</u> my golf swing last week and discovered I was letting the club head dip too far below my shoulders and I wasn't rotating my hips. Now, thanks to his <u>analysis</u>, I am so conscious of my club head and my hips, I can barely hit the ball.

antonym—*n.* the opposite word. *Good* is the <u>antonym</u> of *bad*. *Over* is the <u>antonym</u> of *under*. I have listed <u>antonyms</u> for lots of words throughout this book.

caricature—*n.* a representation of someone with a distinguishing feature exaggerated for effect. A <u>caricature</u> of Jim Carrey would focus on his big, goofy grin and his skinny physique.

characteristics—*n.* special qualities. In Language Arts, physical <u>characteristics</u> usually describe a character in a story or the story's setting. For example, some <u>characteristics</u> of

To remember characteristics, think of the word "character"—characters have characteristics.

Frankenstein include a high, square forehead and rivets coming out of the sides of his head.

chronological—*adj.* in the order events happened. Tests are always asking you to put events in <u>chronological</u> order, or to be able to take a set of <u>chronological</u> events and write a story about them. Jim Carrey's best movies, in chronological order, are *Ace Ventura: Pet Detective* (1994), *Ace Ventura: When Nature Calls* (1995), *Liar Liar* (1997), and *How the Grinch Stole Christmas* (2000).

clarify—*v.* to make clearer. On tests, you will often be asked to <u>clarify</u> sentences and what characters in stories are talking about. *Example*: "Jim Carrey's comedic brilliance over the span of his film career is unsurpassed in the history of cinema" can be <u>clarified</u> as "Jim Carrey is funnier than anyone, ever."

cliché—*n.* a saying that is used too much. For example, it is a <u>cliché</u> to call cafeteria food dog food, because so many people have called it dog food before. In general, when writing a story, you want to avoid using <u>clichés</u>.

coherent—*adj.* making sense. It is important that sentences and paragraphs have a <u>coherent</u> structure. If you are telling a story, the first thing comes first, the second thing comes second, and so on. It is also important for people to be <u>coherent</u>. Newscasters, for instance, have to be <u>coherent</u> so we can understand what they're saying.

Antonym
incoherent—**adj.**
confusing.

complex—*adj.* complicated, made up of a bunch of connected parts. On lots of tests you are asked to read <u>complex</u> passages and find the important information in them. It's like watching a murder mystery on TV and trying to figure out who did it. The mystery is <u>complex</u>, but if you pay attention and concentrate, you can figure out who the culprit is.

Antonym
simple—**adj.**
easy.

compound—*adj.* in Language Arts, a word made of two or more other words is a compound word. *Carpetbagger* (carpet + bagger) is a <u>compound word</u>. (See Social Studies for the definition of *carpetbagger*.) <u>Compound sentences</u> are two sentences connected with a conjunction or a conjunction with a comma.

Example: I really like her, but I am afraid to talk to her.

concise—*adj.* short and to the point. When you are writing, try to be <u>concise</u>. Judge Judy on TV is very concise in her rulings. She usually says something like "You're wrong, you're an idiot, you're guilty!" Now that's <u>concise</u>.

conclusion—*n.* judgment or decision. Many tests ask you what <u>conclusion</u> you can draw from a passage or what <u>conclusion</u> someone in a story came to. That just means you need to be able to sum up what you read. *Example*: After I read the box score from the last Florida Marlins game, I came to the <u>conclusion</u> that they need a few more good hitters. Only three guys on the team are hitting over .300.

conflict—*n.* a clash of ideas; a clash of characters. Most good stories center around <u>conflict</u>—two people who can't stand each other, or two ideas that are really different. *Example*: I am writing a screenplay called *Pretty Dumb* about two actresses who can't stand each other. There is a lot of <u>conflict</u> between the two.

conjunction—*n.* a word that joins words or groups of words in a sentence. There are only a handful of them. The most common are: *and, or, for, but, yet.*

contemporary—*adj.* of this time. In Language Arts, the word is usually used when talking about <u>contemporary</u> writers, which means writers who are writing stuff now. R. L. Stine is a contemporary writer. So is J. K. Rowling.

context—*n.* the setting a word or statement appears in. It's important to know <u>context</u> when you are trying to figure out what someone means. If someone yells "Stop!" the <u>context</u> of that yell tells you why he is yelling. Is his car being stolen? Or is someone going to drive off a cliff? If you know the <u>context</u>, you'll understand what is meant.

contrast—*v.* to find the differences. This word is most often used in test questions that ask you to "compare and <u>contrast</u>." That just means write about the similarities AND the differences. Like: Compare and <u>contrast</u> supermodel/actress James King and actress/pin-up star Pamela Anderson.

credible—*adj.* believable. In a trial, a <u>credible</u> witness is a witness the jury can believe. On a test, a <u>credible</u> answer is one that you think could be true. So if I said Pamela Anderson and James King are both the best actresses in the world, that's not really a <u>credible</u> statement. If I said both are blonde and beautiful—that's <u>credible</u>.

culture—*n.* all of the artistic, scientific, and social accomplishments of a group of people. Basically, everything a group of people does makes up that society's <u>culture</u>. Traditionally, American <u>culture</u> has been summed up as "baseball, hot dogs, and apple pie." I'll agree with the baseball part, but I'm not sure

On the FCAT
Based on the information given, what **conclusion** could you arrive at?

Use all these conjunctions in one loooooong sentence. Come on, it'll be fun! Here, I'll do it first: I ate a peanut butter and jelly sandwich, but I was still hungry, for I hadn't eaten breakfast, so I looked for a cookie, either chocolate chip or oatmeal would do, yet I had a craving for a Rice Krispies Treat. (You can see why run-on sentences are a bad idea.)

To remember credible means "believable," think of incredible, which means "really hard to believe."

about the other two.

dialect—*n.* how a particular part of a country speaks. Where you come from is usually where you get your <u>dialect</u>. Several different <u>dialects</u> can be heard in Florida, including Southern, Midwestern, and even Brooklynese. Authors use <u>dialect</u> in stories to give readers information about character and setting.

dialogue—*n.* the spoken conversations written in a book or a play, usually in quotation marks. Here's some <u>dialogue</u> from *Pretty Dumb*, the screenplay I'm writing for supermodel James King and actress Pamela Anderson. "Hey Pam—my blonde hair is a mess. Poor me. What brand of conditioner do you use?" asked James. "I use Fanteen Selectives, with blonde highlights," Pamela replied, "but you can't borrow it."

editorialize—*v.* to state one's opinion on a subject. Go to the <u>editorial</u> section of your local newspaper for examples of <u>editorializing</u>.

emotional—*adj.* stirred by feelings or emotions. My dad is the <u>emotional</u> one in the family. He even cries during particularly touching Hallmark card commercials.

ethical—*adj.* pertaining to the principles of right and wrong. If you were a movie director, it would not be <u>ethical</u> for you to tell an actress she had a shot to star in your movie if, in fact, you had already offered the job to someone else.

evaluate—*v.* to consider. Tests ask you to <u>evaluate</u> information all of the time. That just means you need to read everything and consider the information before choosing an answer. My mom often <u>evaluates</u> the food she is buying at the grocery store by looking at the ingredients to see how much fat is in it. She hates fat.

expository—*adj.* related to giving forth meaning. An <u>expository</u> statement is a statement that explains the writer's position clearly and in detail. If you are asked to write an <u>expository</u> essay, your teacher wants you to explain or describe your subject in detail.

figurative language—*n.* the use of metaphors. Instead of writing "Dan Marino was a great football player," a sports reporter using <u>figurative language</u> would write "Dan Marino was a football player as great as the Rocky Mountains are tall." (See the definition for *metaphor* for more on this.)

flashback—*n.* a point in a story where the narrative goes back in time for a little while before continuing forward. Books and movies use <u>flashbacks</u> all the time, usually to give you more information about a character or the plot. Sometimes in movies and on TV, they signal a <u>flashback</u> by making the screen get all wiggly or fuzzy.

foreshadow—*v.* to hint at what is to come later in a story.

Remember flashback by thinking of the word "back."

Remember foreshadow by thinking of the word "forward."

A writer may <u>foreshadow</u> that two young characters are going to get married later in the book by having each of them, separately, talk to people about how much they want to get married when they get older.

formal—*adj.* done in a proper way. Think of a <u>formal</u> statement or letter as a statement or letter dressed in a tuxedo. It is stiff, rigid, proper, and perfect. A <u>formal</u> essay is well organized and follows all the rules of grammar and punctuation.

genre—*n.* a type of writing. Romance, horror, mystery, and sci-fi are all fiction <u>genres</u>. My favorite <u>genre</u> is horror, especially R. L. Stine horror.

idiom—*n.* word or phrase that means something it doesn't really mean. Confused? Here are a few <u>idioms</u>:

- *ants in your pants* means *you are fidgety*
- *born with a silver spoon in your mouth* means *your parents are rich*
- *stop bugging me* means *stop bothering me*

imagery—*n.* mental pictures; the use of figurative language to create scenes and moods. Writers use <u>imagery</u> to make their stories more interesting. Here's an example from my screenplay, with the <u>imagery</u> italicized: Pamela Anderson rose from bed and *stretched like a baby bird breaking from its egg*. She had a hard day ahead. She and James King were up for the same part in the new Jim Carrey movie. Whoever got the part would be the toast of the town. Whoever lost would feel *lower than the dirt on the soles of their six-inch stiletto heels*. The movie's director, Fabio, would make his decision soon.

DOUBLE MEANING
interpret—v.
to translate for someone who speaks a different language.

interpret—*v.* to explain. <u>Interpreting</u> is a lot like inferring—it means you consider the information you have and try to figure out what it means.

interview—*n.* a conversation in which one person asks the questions and the other answers. One great way to learn about lots of different people is to read <u>interviews</u> with them in magazines. <u>Interviews</u> can be easier to read than novels and short stories. You can usually read one front-to-back in 30 minutes or less.

irony—*n.* the use of words that mean the opposite of what you mean. A good example is when you say "Gee, I can't wait to go to the dentist and get those cavities filled" in a sarcastic tone, when going to the dentist is obviously the last thing you want to do.

Antonym

figurative—adj.
(see definition.)

literal—*adj.* the real, dictionary meaning. What a word or phrase or any kind of writing or speaking actually means. "Go jump in a lake" usually doesn't mean someone wants you to get wet. But the <u>literal</u> meaning of the phrase is exactly that—go take a leap into the nearest pond, buddy.

logical—*adj*. reasonable. I try to be <u>logical</u> on the golf course. If I hit my drive into the trees, I usually do the <u>logical</u> thing and play it back into the fairway rather than trying to blast a shot through the trees toward the green

metaphor—*n*. figurative use of words in which a word or phrase is used to mean something other than what it really means. As you can probably tell by now, the Language Arts are all about using words in creative ways, just like the fine arts are about using paint and clay in creative ways. For a creative writer, <u>metaphors</u> are as important as paint is for an artist. In my screenplay *Pretty Dumb*, I use metaphors all the time. Here are a couple. Fabio was a filmmaking *machine*, churning out two to three movies a year. Pamela's career was in *overdrive*. Every part she wanted, she got. (See also the definition for *simile*—it's a lot *like* <u>metaphor</u>.)

motivation—*n*. in Language Arts, it is the reason a character does something. Tests often ask you to write down a character's <u>motivation</u>. In my screenplay for *Pretty Dumb*, James King ended up talking about Pamela Anderson behind her back. What was James' <u>motivation</u>? To answer that, you look for the part of the story that made James trash Pamela.

narrative—*n*. a story. The <u>narrative</u> in *Pretty Dumb* follows two actresses as they angle for the starring role in a romantic comedy starring Jim Carrey.

paradox—*n*. a contradiction that is, nonetheless, true. It is truly a <u>paradox</u> that someone who exercises as much as my dad does is incapable of opening a pickle jar without my mom's help. His excuse? He says he has small hands.

paraphrase—*v*. to express something using different words. Tests often ask you to <u>paraphrase</u> a statement or a character's views. That just means restate, in other words, what happened or what was said. I have to be able to paraphrase my screenplay *Pretty Dumb* in just a few words when I go try to sell it to Hollywood. Here it goes: Three days, two blonde actresses, one juicy movie role.

parody—*n*. a humorous mockery. <u>Parodies</u> mimic "normal" writing genres like horror, mystery, and romance. A good movie example of a <u>parody</u> is *The Pink Panther* series, starring Peter Sellers, from the 1960s and '70s. It is a parody of "normal" detective movies. Watch it—you will laugh and laugh and laugh.

perception—*n*. observation. Some people have a false <u>perception</u> of Tiger Woods as an unfeeling, golfing machine. In fact, he is just a normal, happy-go-lucky guy who happens to play golf better than anyone else, ever.

persuade—*v*. to convince. Writers will often try to <u>persuade</u> the readers that their point of view is correct. Tests often ask you

Write the following sentences using metaphors:

Pam is fast.

James is confused.

Fabio likes ice cream a lot.

You can remember paraphrase by thinking of the word "phrase." You are replacing a long piece of writing with a simple phrase.

to figure out what the writer is trying to <u>persuade</u> you to think. I am <u>persuading</u> you to learn the word <u>persuade</u>. <u>Persuaded</u>?

pertinent—*v.* relevant; connected to. In baseball, a player's salary, health, and stats are all <u>pertinent</u> when a trade is being considered.

platitude—*n.* a statement that's a cliché. "The early bird gets the worm" is a <u>platitude</u>. "Slow and steady wins the race" is a <u>platitude</u>.

Write down your favorite (or least favorite) platitude:

_____

_____

_____

point of view—*n.* one way of looking at things. A character's <u>point of view</u> is that character's way of thinking. In my screenplay *Pretty Dumb*, it is James King's <u>point of view</u> that Pamela Anderson is too old for the female lead in a Jim Carrey movie. Pamela Anderson's <u>point of view</u> is that James King is a silly supermodel who would turn the Jim Carrey movie into a disaster. Each tries to persuade the movie's producer, Fabio, that her <u>point of view</u> is the correct one.

On the FCAT

If the story were told from Batman's point of view, which title would be the BEST?

premise—*n.* the basis for a story. The <u>premise</u> of my screenplay *Pretty Dumb* is two blonde actresses are gunning for the same part, and the person who decides who gets the part, Fabio, is evil.

preposition—*n.* a word that relates a noun or a pronoun to the other words in the sentence. Some popular <u>prepositions</u> are: *by, at, to, with, in, for, from.* What's that spell? BATWIFF. (You swing the batt, you whiff.) Remember it.

Write down the premise of the last movie you saw:

_____

_____

_____

_____

_____

preview—*n.* an advance showing. When I go to the movies, my favorite part is the movie <u>previews</u> before the feature presentation. Why? The <u>previews</u> are always good, but the feature presentation is not always good.

propaganda—*n.* the kind of writing that a government or group uses to get you to believe something. <u>Propaganda</u> is used all the time during wars, when one country tells its citizens that the other country is the worst country in the world. And the other country has <u>propaganda</u> that says the same thing about the first country. In propaganda, the facts aren't important—it is convincing readers to believe them that is important.

redundant—*adj.* repetitious. Saying "the great Tiger Woods" is <u>redundant</u>. Everyone already knows he is great.

relevant—*adj.* pertaining to the matter at hand. Tests often tell you to "consider the <u>relevant</u> information" before choosing your answer. You can remember what "relevant" means by thinking of the word "related." <u>Relevant</u> information is "related" to the answer.

resolution—*n.* the end of a story; how something is resolved. If there is a question about a story's resolution, that means the question is about how it ends. I don't want to give away the <u>resolution</u> of my screenplay *Pretty Dumb*, but let's just say there's some hair pulling and a few stiletto heels get broken . . . .

revise—*v.* to edit; to correct and redo. Sometimes you have to <u>revise</u> a report for class. That means edit it and make it clearer. My mom made me <u>revise</u> my screenplay so her favorite singer, Barbra Streisand, could make a cameo appearance.

sensory—*adj.* having to do with the senses. Good video games get players into a state of <u>sensory</u> overload, to where at least three of five senses are fully engaged.

simile—*n.* a comparison that uses the words *like* or *as*. James is crazy <u>like</u> a fox. Pamela is smart <u>as</u> a whip. (By the way—those examples are both also *clichés*.)

speculate—*v.* to think about; to guess at. You are often asked to <u>speculate</u> as to why a character did what he did. That means you need to think about who that character is and why he would do what he did. For example, if you are asked to <u>speculate</u> as to why James King got the part in a movie and Pamela Anderson didn't, you would have to look at the part, why James would be good for it, and why Pamela would not.

summarize—*v.* to create a short recap of the main points of a story. One of the main things you do in Language Arts class is <u>summarize</u> what you read. The best way to write a <u>summary</u> is to recap the story in the order things happened, so you don't forget anything.

suspense—*n.* the state of not knowing what will happen, otherwise known as the thing that puts you on the edge of your seat. Writers use <u>suspense</u> all of the time to keep you turning the pages. If you already know what's going to happen, why read on? In my screenplay, I use <u>suspense</u> the whole way—you don't find out who gets the part in the Jim Carrey movie until the very end.

symbolism—*n.* the use of an object to stand for something that can't be seen. *Example*: There are a lot of statues in Washington, DC, that <u>symbolize</u> the soldiers who lost their lives in our wars. Writers use <u>symbolism</u> when they need to say something without really saying it. An example of this is when a writer <u>symbolizes</u> the passing of seasons by following a leaf as it falls from a tree and then decays on the ground, then feeds the roots of the tree it fell from.

synonym—*n.* a word that means the same thing as another word. *Daring* and *adventurous* are <u>synonyms</u>. *Smart* and *intelligent* are <u>synonyms</u>. When you are writing, instead of using the same word over and over, try to use <u>synonyms</u> to change things up a little bit. So if you use the word *car* in the first sentence, use *automobile* in the second, and *vehicle* in the third.

synonymous—*adj.* alike; having the same meaning, but in a larger sense. Example: Michael Jordan is <u>synonymous</u> with pro basketball. Florida is <u>synonymous</u> with sunshine.

timeline—*n.* a graphical representation of a chronology;

Write a one-sentence summary of the last book you read.

_____
_____
_____
_____

What did the gold medal symbolize for Jackie before she won it?

a bunch of dates in chronological order on a line. <u>Timelines</u> are all over tests. Sometimes you have to write a story from a <u>timeline</u>. Sometimes you have to read a timeline to see what happened in what order. Here's an example from my screenplay:

Pretty Dumb: Monday

10am—James meets with Fabio	3pm—Pamela goes on *Extra* and trashes James	7pm—James and Pamela get in a fight at the Golden Globes
9am—Pamela meets with Fabio	1pm—Pamela and James have lunch	5pm—James goes on *Access Hollywood* and trashes Pamela	11pm—Fabio has a late-night meeting with a mystery actress

universal—*adj.* affecting the whole world. Jim Carrey is <u>universally</u> loved already. After he stars in my movie, that fact will not change.

valid—*adj.* sound. In my screenplay *Pretty Dumb*, Fabio the director has <u>valid</u> reasons to choose James King (she is a star on the rise) and Pamela Anderson (she is a better-known blonde actress). In the end, however, Fabio chooses to put Barbra Streisand in a blonde wig. The movie is a huge hit, Fabio, Barbra, and Jim Carrey all win Oscars, and an angry James King and Pamela Anderson start plotting to ruin Fabio (the plot for *Pretty Dumb II*).

verbal—*adj.* having to do with talking and words. The <u>verbal</u> sections of tests are about words and reading and vocabulary.

analyze
clarify
compare*
contrast*
evaluate
summarize

*These two
words are from
"Test Instructions,"
but are used
most often in
Language Arts.

Language Arts
Thinking Big

Lots of times when you're taking tests, you're asked to write down a date or name that you have memorized. These kinds of test questions basically test your memory. If you remember what you memorized, you'll be just fine.

But sometimes you have to do a little more than just remember. Sometimes you have to really think about a reading passage on a test and figure out on your own what you think and how you should write it down. These kinds of questions ask you to **analyze** a problem, **evaluate** the situation, **summarize** a story, **compare and contrast** ideas, and **clarify** a statement.

When these words appear in test questions, some kids freeze because they know a lot is expected of them—at least a lot more than just writing down a simple definition for a Social Studies test or identifying a shape on a geometry test. A good way to stop yourself from freezing is to get used to **analyzing, evaluating, summarizing,** and **clarifying** in situations that aren't so scary.

One great way to build your vocabulary is to hear the words read aloud. So, until they make an audio version of this book, ask your parents to play an audio book you like when you are driving around. Your local library probably has lots of audio books, just like mine. I personally like to listen to the *Harry Potter* books.

- -

GETTING DEEP EXERCISE

In this exercise you are going to think deep about shallow things that you know a lot about. First, go back to the Language Arts WhizWords and refresh your memory about what the six "Thinking Big" words mean. Now pick a move star, TV star, or entertainer you actually like or know a lot about. I am going to use Britney Spears as my victim, er, subject.

Write your subject at the top of the page. Now write down our six "getting deep" words along the left side of a piece of paper, about five lines apart. Next to each word, write down a topic relating to your victim, er, subject. Then write a short paragraph that answers the "questions" you have written. Here's mine:

Britney Spears

Analyze her album, *Oops... I Did It Again*.
Evaluate her singing.
Summarize why she is so popular.
Clarify her relationship with Justin Timberlake.
Compare and contrast Britney Spears and Christina Aguilera.

Once you have done this with one subject, pick another one and do it again. Keep practicing and you'll get really good at this. The more you see and use these words, the more comfortable you will get with them, and the better you'll do on your tests.

WhizWords

analogy
dialogue
figurative language
flashback
foreshadow
imagery
irony
metaphor
simile
symbolism

Language Arts
Writers' Tools

Good writers know how to use all sorts of tools to keep readers' eyes glued to the page (that's a **metaphor**, by the way). Some writers are so good at it, you just can't stop reading. I keep a flashlight under my bed for nights when my parents tell me to turn out my light and go to sleep, but I just can't stop reading. Good writers make writing look easy, so you don't notice all of the tools they are using.

But on tests, it's important to be able to pick out the tools writers use. Lots of reading questions on tests ask you to identify things like **metaphors, symbolism,** and **analogies**—basically all of the words that I have listed above on this page. The only way to learn how to find all of these things is to practice finding them in the stories you read every day.

IDENTIFYING A WRITER'S TOOLS EXERCISE

You are going to have to do a little hunting and gathering for this exercise. I want you to go through your house and get on the Internet and find examples of the following types of stories:

Newspaper—sports story
Magazine—fashion story
Internet (print one out)—movie review
Newspaper—article from the editorial page
Internet (print one out)—piece of short fiction
Magazine—celebrity profile
Newspaper—political story

Gather these up in one place. Now, over the next week, I want you to read one of these stories every day and:

1. Underline the writers' tools in the text.
2. Identify which writers' tool is used in the margin.

There probably won't be enough room in the margins for some of these. If there isn't, you can write down the writer's tools you identify on Post-It Notes and stick them to the story.

Language Arts
Adverbs and Adjectives

Imagine a world made up of only nouns and verbs. Actors would be . . . just actors. Not terrible actors, not handsome actors, not overpaid actors . . . just actors. Singers would be . . . just singers. Not gorgeous singers or overproduced singers or singers with voices that only a mother could love. Just . . . singers.

Luckily we have adverbs and adjectives, the words that make life special! Tiger Woods is the <u>best</u> golfer ever. He has a <u>sweet</u> swing, <u>lethal</u> putting stroke, and <u>steely</u> nerves. All other golfers fear him, but <u>lefty</u> Phil Mickelson and the <u>determined</u> David Duval may still find what it takes to beat him some day.

Yes, <u>adjectives</u> and <u>adverbs</u>, the simple modifiers of verbs, nouns, and other adjectives and adverbs, give writing its spice. So it is very important to use them when you write. It makes your writing more interesting to read, which gets you better grades on your papers and writing tests. All good things, wouldn't you say?

WRITING YOUR AUTOBIOGRAPHY EXERCISE

If you don't believe me, let me prove it. I want you to try to describe your own life without adjectives and adverbs. Then I want you to describe your life WITH adjectives and adverbs—as many as you can possibly think of.

That's right—it's autobiography time. Grab a pencil and paper. Start by filling out this general outline. Write down three events in each age bracket you will write about in your own journal or notebook. Stuff like losing your first tooth, learning to swim, moving to a new town, joining the basketball team—events that are memorable and important to you.

Age

0-4 _____

5-8 _____

9-present _____

Now write two versions of your autobiography: 1) using no adverbs or adjectives; and 2) using as many adverbs and adjectives as you can think of. Underline the adjectives and adverbs in the second version when you are done. I have provided you with a few adjectives and adverbs that you can use if you get stumped.

Adjectives and Adverbs for Your Autobiography
goofy
fast
unbelievable
slow
smelly
late
first
early
straight
green
gawky
crazy
fun
laughable
smart
right
heavenly
regrettable

Chapter 2

Social Studies

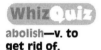

abolish—v. to get rid of.

abolitionist—*n.* someone who fought against slavery. When this country had slavery, there were a bunch of <u>abolitionists</u> trying to free the slaves. Some gave speeches, some ran the underground railroad—all of the <u>abolitionists</u> were working to stop an immoral system.

accelerate—*v.* to speed up. You often see this word when people are discussing tensions around the world. Example: Peace talks have <u>accelerated</u> since the leaders agreed to work on a new treaty.

adapt—*v.* to change in response to one's surroundings. The word is often used to describe how people and animals <u>adapt</u> as the environment changes. Charles Darwin found that animals <u>adapt</u> to their environments. When my little sister was born, I had to <u>adapt</u> to all the attention she was getting.

adversary—*n.* the enemy! President George W. Bush's <u>adversary</u> in the 2000 presidential election was Al Gore.

Name three rules at school that you advocate.
1. _____
2. _____
3. _____

advocate—*n.* someone who supports a cause. My mom is a big <u>advocate</u> of the new dress code at school because she doesn't have to buy me expensive clothes anymore—just blue pants and a white shirt. If you <u>advocate</u> something, you support it.

aggressor—*n.* the person or country who attacks first. Germany was the <u>aggressor</u> in World War II.

agitator—*n.* someone who stirs things up to bring about change. <u>Agitators</u> are usually described as rebellious and loudmouthed. Abbie Hoffman was an anti-war <u>agitator</u> during the Vietnam War. He led demonstrations and protests against the war.

industrial—adj. an economy based on manufacturing (building things).

agrarian—*adj.* pertaining to a culture or economy based on farming and agriculture. The U.S. went from an <u>agrarian</u> economy in the 1800s to an industrial economy in the 1900s. Now there are hardly any farmers left.

allegiance—*n.* a deep commitment to something, like your

20

country or your family. Of course, we have all pledged <u>allegiance</u> to the flag in school.

alliance—*n.* an association of people or nations coming together to achieve a common goal. Think of the TV show *Survivor*—the players try to form <u>alliances</u> to protect themselves from getting voted off the show.

Related Word

ally—n. friend; someone in an alliance.

ambition—*n.* a burning desire to achieve a goal or to become something. Madonna is often noted for her <u>ambition</u> to become famous. She doesn't have much singing talent, just tons of <u>ambition</u>. The same can be said of lots of actors and politicians.

amendment—*n.* a change to the Constitution. We have had 27 <u>amendments</u> since the Constitution was written in 1789.

Related Word

amend—v. to correct or fix something.

anarchy—*n.* the state of having no government—or anyone else—in charge. <u>Anarchy</u> is usually thought of as a bad thing, with bands of hoodlums running around in the street, breaking windows, and beating people up. Sometimes after a team wins the World Series or the NBA Championship, there is <u>anarchy</u> in the streets when their fans go nuts and start turning over cars and lighting fires.

annex—*v.* to attach or join. You usually hear this word used in situations where a new piece of land is attached to land already owned. Countries <u>annex</u> other countries (usually after they win a war); cities <u>annex</u> surrounding suburbs.

arduous—*adj.* extremely hard or difficult. The word is often used when describing the <u>arduous</u> journey of U.S. settlers west. They could only go a few miles a day in their wagon trains, Native Americans were always attacking them, they got sick and died because there were no doctors, and they didn't even really know what was waiting for them where they were going. Now that's <u>arduous</u>.

Whiz Quiz

Write down your three most arduous classes in school.
1. _____
2. _____
3. _____

assert—*v.* to claim; to insist. The colonies <u>asserted</u> their independence from England. They just went and claimed it, no questions asked. During the Civil Rights movement, African

Social Studies

Americans <u>asserted</u> their right to vote. In the '70s, feminists <u>asserted</u> their right to equal pay for equal work. As citizens, we <u>assert</u> our rights to do things all the time—no one can stop us. Yes, you could call this country <u>Assert</u>america if you wanted!

DOUBLE MEANING
assimilate—v.
when the body breaks food down into its nutrients (science).

assimilate—*v.* to make similar or to absorb into a system or culture. This word is often used when discussing how immigrants are absorbed into American culture. <u>Assimilation</u> is a complex process. Immigrants come here with their own customs. They want to keep some customs, but they also need to adopt some American customs. So the country <u>assimilates</u> them, but it is never easy.

One way to remember benevolent is to imagine a nice person named Ben: like Ben Franklin or Ben Affleck.

benevolent—*adj.* kind; caring. Most often used when talking about a "<u>benevolent</u> dictator," which means the dictator has total power, but he uses it for good, not evil. Superman would be a <u>benevolent</u> dictator.

bias—*n.* prejudice. It usually means thinking someone is less than you are for a reason that doesn't make any sense, like gender, and skin color. That is <u>bias</u>, or prejudice.

boom and bust economy—*n.* a kind of economy where things go incredibly well for a while, then crash and go incredibly poorly from there on out. It is most often used to describe the California gold rush in the 1800s, when everyone flocked to California for the <u>boom</u>, but once everyone was there and all of the gold had been mined, it all went <u>bust</u>.

bourgeoisie—*n.* the middle class. The <u>bourgeoisie</u> is mentioned all of the time when you are studying communism. For a communist, the <u>bourgeoisie</u> is the enemy of the proletariat (the working class).

boycott—*v.* to refuse to have dealings with a company or country because you disagree with something it does. It is a peaceful way to protest. Instead of picketing or doing something violent, people can <u>boycott</u>. Martin Luther King convinced black people to <u>boycott</u> of the Montgomery, Alabama, bus system to protest segregation on the buses. That meant no black people would ride the buses, which meant the buses lost a lot of money. So then they had to pay attention to what Martin Luther King said, or they would go out of business.

capitalism—*n.* an economic system where the means of production (capital) are privately owned. The United States is a <u>capitalist</u> country, where people own the businesses and land. Donald Trump is a famous <u>capitalist</u>.

The term carpetbagger was used to describe Northerners who moved South after the Civil War with nothing but the contents of their carpet-bags (suitcases) to take advantage of the post-war chaos to enter politics.

carpetbagger—*n.* a politician who runs for office in a state she is not from. Most recently, Hillary Rodham Clinton was called a <u>carpetbagger</u> when she ran for elected office in New

York, even though she was not from New York and had never lived there before, either.

cede—*v.* to give up. When a country loses a war, it often has to <u>cede</u> some land to the victor.

censorship—*n.* restriction on what someone can say or do. Although the First Amendment to the Constitution protects our right to freedom of speech, television shows are <u>censored</u>, movies are <u>censored</u>, and songs are <u>censored</u>. It happens every day in this country—usually to protect young people from adult language and situations. Many artists and performers are frustrated by censorship in the United States. Some countries, however, <u>censor</u> everyone on what they can say anywhere, anytime. This type of <u>censorship</u> is used to control people and prevent them from complaining about the government.

centralized—*adj.* focused in one person or area. In Social Studies, the word is usually used to talk about governments. A <u>centralized</u> government gives a lot of power to one person or group of people—like a king or a single ruling party.

checks and balances—*n.* when talking about the U.S. government, it is the system of government in which each branch limits the powers of the other two branches. So the president can do some things, but Congress has a say in what he does. Same with Congress—it can do some things, but the president also has a say. The judiciary branch—the courts—has a say in everything, too, and Congress and the president have a say in who gets to be a judge.

chivalry—*n.* qualities idealized by knighthood, like bravery, honor, and benevolence. Once, my mom was getting yelled at in the grocery store by some guy who claimed she took his head of iceberg lettuce. I stood up for her and told the guy to stuff it. My mom then yelled "<u>Chivalry</u> is not dead!" That was an exciting day at the grocery store.

civic—*adj.* relating to your city or town. This word is sometimes used when discussing your role as a citizen. People often say "It's your <u>civic</u> duty to vote." That just means that as a member of a community, you should take part in what is going on there.

civil disobedience—*n.* a kind of protest where someone refuses to obey civil laws because she doesn't believe in them. <u>Civil disobedience</u> is almost always nonviolent. Martin Luther King organized sit-ins to protest "whites-only" restaurants. Black people would simply sit at a table and not leave until the cops came and took them away.

coerce—*v.* to force someone to do something by threatening him. I was <u>coerced</u> into babysitting for my sister last weekend—my dad said if I didn't, I wouldn't get the new PlayStation—

Antonym

decentralized—adj. A decentralized government spreads out power to a lot of people or groups of people.

WhizFact

The American writer Henry David Thoreau is the one who coined the term civil disobedience in the late 19th century.

ever! You may have heard about the <u>Coercive Acts</u> that England forced on the American colonies (called the Intolerable Acts by the colonists) after the Boston Tea Party.

colonize—*v.* to establish a culture in a foreign land by putting some citizens there. <u>Colonization</u> often results in those citizens taking over that foreign land. It's not a very nice thing to do, but it has been a common practice for many countries, including the United States.

commerce—*n.* the act of buying and selling things. When you go to Wal-Mart and buy a notebook, you are engaging in <u>commerce</u>, and so is Wal-Mart.

commodity—*n.* something that is bought or sold. Like a notebook or a car or a ton of grain. They are all <u>commodities</u>.

communism—*n.* a system where the people own the factories, farms, and other property. At least that is the <u>communist</u> ideal. In most <u>communist</u> countries so far—like Cuba and the old Soviet Union—the government "owns" the property and most of the people have little say in how everything is run.

compensation—*n.* the amount paid for goods (stuff) or services (labor). When you get paid for doing something, you are getting <u>compensation</u>. When you pay for something, you are giving <u>compensation</u>.

compromise—*n.* a settlement where each side gives up something. So if you want to watch TV after dinner but your dad wants you to wash the dishes, a <u>compromise</u> would be watching TV, then washing the dishes afterward.

concession—*n.* something that is given up. When I wanted to switch bedrooms with my big sister Jenny, I offered a series of <u>concessions</u>: I would do her laundry, I would bow low whenever she came into a room, and I would give her my dessert for a whole year. She didn't budge.

confederation—*n.* a group of people, states, or countries who join together to do something. The Confederacy in the Civil War was a <u>confederation</u> of slave-owning states in the South.

confiscate—*v.* to take away. Once my parents <u>confiscated</u> my PlayStation for one month because I got three straight Cs in Language Arts class. I still have not forgiven them.

conquistador—*n.* a Spanish conqueror. Hernando de Soto was a <u>conquistador</u>. He was commissioned by Spain in the 16th century to conquer what is now Florida.

conscription—*n.* the policy of forcing citizens to fight in wars. It's also called the draft. At different points in history, America has <u>conscripted</u> people into the armed forces, usually when there

---

was a war on. At other times, the armed forces have been made up of volunteers.

consensus—*n.* general agreement. After my sister Jenny refused to switch bedrooms with me, I tried to form a <u>consensus</u> among the rest of my family (parents, grandparents, cousins, uncles, aunts) that I deserved her room. While I succeeded, and they agreed with me, she still wouldn't budge.

consent—*n.* permission. In Social Studies, it is often used to describe elected officials serving at the "<u>consent</u> of the governed." That means we put them in office by voting for them, and we can get rid of them if we want.

consequences—*n.* the results of something that happened. As a parent or teacher must have told you at some point in your life, there are <u>consequences</u> for your actions. In Social Studies, the word is usually used when talking about something bad that happened, like Japan bombing Pearl Harbor (<u>consequences</u>: the U.S. joined the war) or the Watergate scandal (<u>consequences</u>: Nixon resigned). But <u>consequences</u> can also stem from positive events.

constituent—*n.* a member of a group that is represented by an elected official. In a democracy, politicians are supposed to do the bidding of their <u>constituents</u>. If they don't, their <u>constituents</u> can elect someone else who will.

constitution—*n.* the laws that govern a group of people, usually a country or state. The U.S. <u>Constitution</u> has in it the basic laws that we follow in this country.

contraband—*n.* stolen or illegal goods. Once at school the principal checked all of our lockers because he said he had reports that someone was hiding <u>contraband</u>. He didn't find anything, so I guess his sources were not good.

controversy—*n.* a situation where two sides have opposing views, and people have a hard time figuring out who is right. There was a huge <u>controversy</u> at my school last year when my friend Ralph refused to wear the new uniform—and his parents agreed with him! The principal called an assembly, Ralph's parents were in and out of school almost every day, Ralph was suspended, and it was in the newspaper!

cultivate—*v.* to tend land for the purpose of growing crops. Once for a science project I had to <u>cultivate</u> a one-square-meter plot of land behind our school. I planted beans.

corrupt—*v.* marked by dishonesty. The history of the United States is filled with <u>corrupt</u> politicians—politicians who took bribes to get laws passed.

currency—*n.* a country's money. Our <u>currency</u> is dollars, the British use pounds, and the Japanese use yen.

Social Studies

debate—*v.* to argue. During the last presidential election my parents were both glued to the television for the presidential <u>debates</u>, which meant I couldn't use my PlayStation. Needless to say, I was not happy.

democracy—*n.* a government where the people hold the power. We have a representative <u>democracy</u>, which means we elect representatives to do what we, the people, want them to do.

despotism—*n.* rule by a despot, someone who has absolute power and can do whatever he wants. Hitler was a <u>despot</u> in Germany. Saddam Hussein is a <u>despot</u> in Iraq. There are still lots of <u>despots</u> around the world.

Whiz Tip

To remember **despotism, think** of the word "despicable."

deter—*v.* to prevent; to stop. My mom doesn't understand why Britney Spears' mom doesn't try to <u>deter</u> her from wearing those skimpy outfits onstage.

Related Word

diplomatic—adj. good at dealing with people and their problems.

diplomat—*n.* a person who represents her country while living in another country. Most countries have <u>diplomats</u> in other countries, so if something happens, say, in Mexico, the United States' <u>diplomat</u> in Mexico can make sure the United States' interests are kept in mind.

DOUBLE MEANING
discriminate—v. to tell one thing from another. Example: I can't **discriminate** between these two cheeses: Which one is Swiss?

discriminate—*v.* to treat someone badly for unfair reasons. Black people have been <u>discriminated</u> against a lot in our country. Even my favorite sport, baseball, <u>discriminated</u> against black people until 1947, when Jackie Robinson became the first black man in the Major Leagues. And racial <u>discrimination</u> still exists—there may be tons of black players, but there are hardly any black managers.

displace—*v.* to move out of place; to remove. When one people or country invade another land, the people who already live there are usually <u>displaced</u>.

dissent—*n.* disagreement. In America, you have the right to register your <u>dissent</u>, no matter what you think. It's called freedom of speech. My friend Ralph's parents had every right to register their <u>dissent</u> with the school's dress code. They lost—Ralph had to wear the uniform like the rest of us, but they still had the right to disagree.

DOUBLE MEANING
diversity—n.
a variety of plants and animals in an ecosystem (science).

diversity—*n.* variety. In Social Studies, the word is usually used to talk about the <u>diversity</u> of opinions (lots of different opinions) and the <u>diversity</u> of cultures (lots of different cultures) that make up America. Some call our <u>diversity</u> a melting pot, some call it a quilt—the point is, we have a very <u>diverse</u> society.

Antonym

foreign—adj. having to do with other countries or lands.

domestic—*adj.* having to do with home. In Social Studies, you may hear the phrase "<u>domestic</u> affairs"—that refers to issues within a country, not in other countries.

dominate—*v.* to take precedence; to be most important.

Combining the definition above with this one, you may have heard of "domestic affairs <u>dominating</u> Congress" or something along those lines. That means issues close to home are taking up most of the time and effort in Congress. Different issues tend to <u>dominate</u> in our culture, depending on all sorts of things: war and peace, the economy, the rights of people being respected or abused. All of these issues have <u>dominated</u> at one time or another.

due process—*n.* the established way our court system works. The phrase "You have a right to <u>due process</u>" is very important in this country. It means no matter who you are, you get treated the same—and fairly—in our court system.

economy—*n.* the combination of goods, services, and people and how they all work together to survive. We have a market <u>economy</u>, which means the laws of supply and demand determines who makes and gets what. The other kind of <u>economy</u> is a command <u>economy</u>, where a government determines (commands) who makes and gets what. China has a command <u>economy</u>.

eligible—*adj.* qualified; available. An <u>eligible</u> voter is someone who is qualified to vote—this person is a citizen, has registered, is old enough, etc. An <u>eligible</u> bachelor is someone who is not married or dating anyone and would make somebody a good husband. I am an <u>eligible</u> bachelor.

eloquent—*adj.* good at public speaking. If you are a politician, it helps to be <u>eloquent</u>, since you have to make so many speeches all the time. John F. Kennedy was an <u>eloquent</u> speaker; so were Ronald Reagan and Bill Clinton. But I think the most <u>eloquent</u> speaker I know is the Rock on *WWF Smackdown*. That guy can really hold an audience!

emancipation—*n.* the act of gaining freedom. Our <u>emancipation</u> from England and the <u>emancipation</u> of slaves in our country are two pivotal moments in our history.

emigrate—*v.* to leave one's home country for another. This country is made up of millions of people who have <u>emigrated</u> from distant lands to find opportunity here. Orlando Hernandez is a major league pitcher who <u>emigrated</u> from Cuba.

entrepreneur—*n.* someone who takes business risks in a capitalist economy. In other words, someone who bets that if she is right about a business venture, she will get rich. <u>Entrepreneurs</u> start most of the new companies in our country every year, each betting their businesses will succeed. Steve Jobs was an <u>entrepreneur</u> when he started Apple Computer in his garage in the 1970s. Martha Stewart took an ability to make pretty doilies and turned it into a multimillion dollar empire!

epidemic—*n.* an outbreak of a contagious disease. There is currently an AIDS <u>epidemic</u>, with millions of people infected

DOUBLE MEANING
economy—n. the careful, thrifty use of something. "She skates with economy of movement" means she doesn't waste any motion.

The U.S. is called "the land of the free," so emancipation (freedom) is probably our most important ideal. That means you are lucky—but it also means lots of test questions on the subject.

● and thousands dying every year.

executive branch—*n.* the branch of government that administers the country. The president is the head of the <u>executive branch</u>.

expansion—*n.* growth. As in territorial <u>expansion</u>, it means a country keeps annexing the land that is next to it, and then the land next to that. The U.S. <u>expanded</u> from 13 states on the East Coast all the way west to California, and then picked up Alaska and Hawaii, too. Now that's what I call <u>expansion</u>.

exploit—*v.* to take advantage of. As part of my plan to get my sister's bedroom, I tried to <u>exploit</u> her main weakness: she loves Justin Timberlake. I told her I would get her 'N Sync tickets if she would trade bedrooms with me. Jenny laughed and called me a little doofus. This is definitely war.

exterminate—*v.* to eradicate; to get rid of. To remember this word, think of the <u>exterminator</u> who comes to get rid of termites, mice, or roaches.

extract—*v.* to take from. If I can <u>extract</u> one lesson from my struggles with my sister, it is this: Girls are hard to understand.

fascism—*n.* a government with a ruthless dictator, centralized control, and nationalist tendencies. Hitler was a <u>fascist</u>. So was Mussolini. The Allied Powers fought <u>fascism</u> in World War II and won. It's all my great-grandfather talks about!

federalism—*n.* a government with separate states that are united under one larger government. The United States (get it—*united* states) is a <u>federalist</u> system. Alexander Hamilton was an advocate of <u>federalism</u>.

feminism—*n.* a movement committed to getting women the same rights and opportunities as men. Women make less money than men for the same work, and our society treats them differently in many ways. <u>Feminists</u> are out to change that so everyone is equal.

feudalism—*n.* an economic system in Europe that lasted throughout the Middle Ages in which subjects had to serve their lords.

forfeit—*v.* to give up; to hand over. When someone commits a crime and goes to jail, he <u>forfeits</u> a lot of his rights as a citizen, like the freedom to walk around and go wherever he wants. If your baseball team doesn't show up for a game, it <u>forfeits</u> the game, and loses automatically. That happened to my team when our bus broke down.

fortitude—*n.* strength. My sister Jenny is showing great <u>fortitude</u> as I try to wear her down and get her to switch bedrooms with me. There must be something I can do to make her change her mind.

Whiz Fact

Gloria Steinem and Betty Friedan are famous modern feminists. Elizabeth Cady Stanton is a famous suffragette —a woman who fought for women's right to vote in the early 20th century (see definition for suffrage).

Whiz Tip

To remember fortitude, think of how *forts* are built to be strong so the dudes inside can have a lot of *'tude.*

free enterprise—*n.* an economic system in which businesses can try to make a profit without the government getting in their way with lots of regulations. The United States has a <u>free enterprise</u> system.

fundamental—*adj.* basic. In this country we have certain <u>fundamental</u> rights—the rights to life, liberty, and the pursuit of happiness. Maybe you've heard of these somewhere?

futile—*adj.* useless. Lots of times people will tell you not to try, that trying is <u>futile</u>. Until the Magic got Tracy McGrady, I thought the team's attempts to get to the playoffs were <u>futile</u>. Now, I think they could win the NBA championship.

grievances—*n.* complaints. The colonists had a list of <u>grievances</u> against mother England, the biggest of which was they were getting taxed a lot. I have a list of <u>grievances</u> I gave to my mother last week, the biggest of which was my allowance needs to be higher. The colonists rebelled. I hope my mom gets the hint!

harass—*v.* to bother over and over and over again. I tried <u>harassing</u> my sister to give me her room. Every morning at breakfast I peppered her with questions about why she deserved the big room and I deserved the small room. My <u>harassment</u> strategy backfired when she started taking her breakfast to her room.

hazardous—*adj.* dangerous. You've probably seen this word in ads for cigarettes: "CAUTION: cigarette smoking may be <u>hazardous</u> to your health." Being an early colonist was also definitely <u>hazardous</u> to one's health.

hostile—*adj.* angry. Sometimes on *Judge Judy* the plaintiffs and defendants get <u>hostile</u> with each other. That's when Judge Judy usually steps in and tells them to put a sock in it.

humane—*adj.* kind and gentle. I've probably seen 50 episodes of *Judge Judy* and I wouldn't describe her as being especially <u>humane</u>. She practices what my mom calls "tough love."

iconoclast—*n.* one who goes against the norm and aims to overthrow traditional ideas or institutions. Some people called Ralph Nader an <u>iconoclast</u> because he ran for president against the big boys—the Democrats and the Republicans in 2000.

idealist—*n.* one who is more influenced by a pursuit of perfection than by practicalities. An <u>idealist</u> wants to do what is right, no matter how hard or impractical it may be.

immigration—*n.* the act of coming from a foreign country to live in a new country. America has grown in population over the years mainly due to <u>immigration</u>. The country practically begged

Whiz Quiz

List three things you once thought were futile:

1. _____
2. _____
3. _____

29

people to <u>immigrate</u> here so it could push west over the frontier and fill up all of its land with new citizens.

impartial—*adj.* fair. Judges and juries are supposed to be <u>impartial</u>. That means they just go by the facts. Like Judge Judy on TV—she is an <u>impartial</u> judge who listens to all the facts, then she reams the person who is guilty.

Who was the first president to be impeached? Hint: it wasn't Bill Clinton.

impeachment—*n.* charging an elected official with doing something wrong. President Clinton was <u>impeached</u> a few years ago. It was only the second time in the history of the country a president was <u>impeached</u>. Clinton's <u>impeachment</u> hearings dominated the news for weeks.

imperialism—*n.* rule by an empire. A few hundred years ago, <u>imperialism</u> was the way to go. There was the Roman Empire, the Spanish Empire, the German Empire. These <u>imperial</u> governments would go out and conquer a bunch of countries so they could expand their empires. Of course America was part of the British Empire—<u>imperial</u> Britain—at one point.

DOUBLE MEANING

impose v.—to butt in. You may have heard people say "I don't mean to impose, but . . ." and then they go ahead and impose.

impose—*v.* to force. My Spanish teacher <u>imposed</u> a "no English" rule last week in class, so no one could speak English in her class the whole week! If you did, you had to put your head on your desk for five minutes. It was really funny watching everyone mess up and put their heads on their desks.

inalienable—*adj.* unable to be taken away; unable to be separated from. Most often linked to Americans' <u>inalienable</u> rights to life, liberty, and the pursuit of happiness. One way to remember this word is to think about the word "alien." Space aliens are beings from other planets. So something that is *inalienable* is something that is *not* something from another planet.

inaugurate—*v.* to have a ceremony where a politician gets installed in office. George W. Bush was <u>inaugurated</u> in 2001 after a bitter election battle against Al Gore.

indigenous—*adj.* native. The people who are originally from a country are called the country's <u>indigenous</u> people. Native Americans are <u>indigenous</u> to North America—everyone else who lives in this country came here from somewhere else or is descended from someone who did.

industrialism—*n.* an economic system where big industries are most important. <u>Industrialism</u> dominated the United States in the 20th century.

inevitable—*adj.* going to happen; unavoidable. It is <u>inevitable</u> that you are going to have to take tests, so you might as well just get used to them. When something is unavoidable, my grandfather always says "It's as <u>inevitable</u> as death and taxes." I have my own expression, "It's as <u>inevitable</u> as death, taxes, and the FCAT."

influence—*n.* the power to change something. The United States has incredible <u>influence</u> around the world due to our economic and military might. In 1936, a man named Dale Carnegie wrote a book called *How to Win Friends and <u>Influence</u> People*, and it became one of the best-selling books of all time because, well, that's what everyone wants, right?

inhabitants—*n.* people who live somewhere. You are an <u>inhabitant</u> of Florida. Prince Charles is an <u>inhabitant</u> of England.

innovation—*n.* a brand new way of doing something; a new device that is better than the previous device. The electric guitar was an <u>innovation</u> that allowed bands to play louder. Before the electric guitar, the only way to play loud was on an acoustic guitar aimed at a microphone.

Related Word
innovate—v. to introduce something new.

instability—*n.* the quality of being unsteady or insecure. When things are up in the air, when they can go one way or the other— that is <u>instability</u>. *Example*: There is <u>instability</u> on a baseball team when the players don't like the manager and the manager doesn't like the players. Who is right—the players who say the manager is stupid or the manager who says the players are terrible? Who do you side with? All these questions lead to <u>instability</u>. It's the same with a country when there is <u>instability</u>. Usually, there is <u>instability</u> when there is a change in leaders. Maybe the army liked the old leader better, so they won't listen to the new leader. That leads to <u>instability</u>.

insurgent—*n.* a person who revolts against authority. When you watch newscasters, you may hear them talk about "rebel <u>insurgents</u>" in other countries, and then show some guys with machine guns running around in the woods fighting against government forces.

insurrection—*n.* revolt against the people in charge. The word is used in the Declaration of Independence to describe the king of England's treatment of the colonies: "He has excited domestic <u>insurrections</u> amongst us." That means the colonists thought the king was turning them against each other.

**Famous insurgents
include civil
rights leader
Martin Luther
King, Jr., our third
president Thomas
Jefferson, and
the poet Allen
Ginsberg. They all
went against
authority.**

integration—*n.* the creation of one group by combining different groups; having people of all different races living together instead of apart. Our country was segregated—white people and black people were separated from each other until the 1950s and 1960s, when segregation was made illegal. Now we are an <u>integrated</u> society—people of all races are allowed to live side by side.

integrity—*n.* honesty; trustworthiness. People who do what they say they are going to do have <u>integrity</u>. People who lie do not have <u>integrity</u>. I think Justin Timberlake has <u>integrity</u>

for staying with 'N Sync, even though he could go solo and make millions.

Think of the word "depend" to remember interdependent.

interdependent—*adj.* depending on each other. Countries are getting more and more <u>interdependent</u>. Lots of countries rely on us for corn; we rely on lots of countries for oil; and everyone relies on France for French fries.

intervene—*v.* to butt in. I had to <u>intervene</u> on the playground last week when my friend Ralph and that jerk Frankie got into a fight. I was able to keep them apart until the teacher came.

intolerant—*adj.* unable to accept views one doesn't agree with. There are lots of intolerant people in the world—people who don't like other people just because they are different. Don't be <u>intolerant</u>. It will just make you mean.

isolate—*v.* to separate from everything else. When I was in kindergarten, I was a big spaz. Sometimes I got so hyper my teacher had to <u>isolate</u> me at nap time—she put up big dividers so I couldn't see the rest of the kids and they couldn't see me.

jeopardy—*n.* peril; danger. Think of the game show *Jeopardy*. If you go on that show, you are in <u>jeopardy</u> of looking really stupid if you can't answer any questions.

judicial branch—*n.* the country's court system. One of three branches of the U.S. government, the <u>judicial branch</u> interprets the laws and hands down punishments.

jurisdiction—*n.* an area of authority. The word <u>jurisdiction</u> is often used to talk about the courts having <u>jurisdiction</u> over a case. That means the case happened in a court's physical area. So if someone robbed someone in Palm Beach County, the case would be tried in the <u>jurisdiction</u> of Palm Beach County.

lame duck—*n.* a politician who has some time left in her term, but her replacement has already been elected. So she is still doing her job, but she has already been voted out. That means she has no power, and she's basically just keeping the seat warm for her successor.

legislative branch—*n.* the branch of government that writes the laws. The U.S. has a bicameral <u>legislative branch</u> made up of the House of Representatives and the Senate.

loyalist—*n.* someone who is loyal to a leader or government. British <u>loyalists</u> who lived in the American colonies were against the colonies breaking from mother England.

Related Word

landslide—n. winning an election by a huge margin.

mandate—*n.* the right to do something. In elections, when voters pick someone overwhelmingly, that politician has a <u>mandate</u>. That means the voters have told him—with their votes—that he can do what he wants because they agree with his plan. When a politician wins in a landslide (see the Related Word) he has a <u>mandate</u> from the voters. When there is a close election (like when George W. Bush barely beat Al Gore in 2000), there is not a <u>mandate</u> because lots of people voted for the guy who lost.

manifest destiny—*n.* a policy of imperialist expansion that says a country can take over another country because God says so. Imperialist countries like England took over other countries using this concept of <u>manifest destiny</u>. The United States took over lots of its western lands by using this concept of <u>manifest destiny</u>. <u>Manifest destiny</u> is bad. It's basically just an excuse to take over a country.

mercenary—*n.* a professional soldier. <u>Mercenaries</u> fight for whomever pays them to fight. There's even a magazine for <u>mercenaries</u> called *Soldier of Fortune*. Get it? They *soldier* so they can make a *fortune*.

migration—*n.* the movement from one place to another. In the past 20 years, there has been a <u>migration</u> of people in this country from cold places like New York to warm places like Florida.

militant—*adj.* combative; warring. Some countries have <u>militant</u> histories, ours included.

moderate—*adj.* not extreme. <u>Moderate</u> temperatures are not too hot and not too cold. <u>Moderate</u> politicians are not too liberal and not too conservative.

municipal—*adj.* related to a city or a town. You probably have heard of a <u>municipal</u> government and a <u>municipal</u> school system and <u>municipal</u> courts. That just means those things are located in a city—whatever city that may be.

mutual—*adj.* shared in common between two people, groups, or things. When something is done for <u>mutual</u> benefit, that means both parties benefit. When Justin Timberlake and Britney Spears are seen in public together, they <u>mutually</u> benefit. All of her fans start to like him, and all of his fans start to like her.

nationalism—*n.* loyalty to one's country. <u>Nationalism</u> is a good thing when it means you really like your country and are proud of it. <u>Nationalism</u> is a bad thing when it means you really like your country but hate all the other countries. Most often these days, when you hear about <u>nationalism</u>, it's when one country is beating up on another one out of a feeling of <u>nationalism</u>.

naturalization—*n.* the granting of citizenship to someone. The word is most often used when discussing the INS—the Immigration and <u>Naturalization</u> Service. That is the agency that helps people immigrate to this country and become citizens. A <u>naturalized</u> citizen is someone who immigrated here and became a citizen later.

DOUBLE MEANING
moderate—**v.**
to manage a group of people who have different views.

The scientist Albert Einstein once said "Nationalism is an infantile sickness. It is the measles of the human race."

Social Studies

negotiate—*v.* to discuss something with the goal of reaching an agreement. Throughout history there have basically been two ways to solve disagreements—to fight or to <u>negotiate</u>. <u>Negotiating</u> is better because nobody gets hurt.

Name your nemesis!

_____

nemesis—*n.* sworn enemy. The Joker is Batman's <u>nemesis</u>. Lex Luthor is Superman's <u>nemesis</u>. Christina Aguilera is Britney Spears' <u>nemesis</u>. The Soviet Union used to be the United States' <u>nemesis</u>.

Synonym

impartial—adj. fair.

neutral—*adj.* not taking sides. Lots of times, when two countries go to war, other countries remain <u>neutral</u>. That means they aren't taking sides in the war—they are staying out of it. The United States was <u>neutral</u> in World War II until Japan bombed Pearl Harbor.

nullify—*v.* to void; to take something back. Sometimes, after an agreement has been negotiated, something happens and the agreement gets <u>nullified</u>. That means all the negotiating was wasted, because the agreement that was reached doesn't count. It happens all the time in baseball when a team is trying to make a trade, but the trade gets <u>nullified</u> when one of the players doesn't pass his physical.

obstacle—*n.* something that gets in the way. You have probably been in a race through an <u>obstacle</u> course at some point. My main <u>obstacle</u> at school is that I have a hard time paying attention, but I'm working on it.

opportunity—*n.* chance. The United States has been called "the land of <u>opportunity</u>." And my dad is always saying "When <u>opportunity</u> knocks—open the door!" He loves that one.

Name your favorite team's main opposition:

_____

opposition—*n.* someone who is against someone else. It looks like the Heat's main <u>opposition</u> this year as they try to get to the NBA Finals is going to be the Philadelphia 76ers.

oppress—*v.* to keep somebody down. This country has a history of <u>oppressing</u> black people and women. That <u>oppression</u> isn't nearly as bad now as it used to be.

WhizTip

To remember orator think of "oral"—having to do with the mouth (speaking).

orator—*n.* someone who gives speeches. It is important for a politician to be a good <u>orator</u>, because he has to give speeches that convince people to vote for him. President Bush is NOT a good <u>orator</u>—he can barely string together two sentences.

partisan—*n.* a supporter of a political party; a supporter of a cause. You have probably heard of "<u>partisan</u> politics" in Washington, DC. That means our two major political parties—the Democrats and Republicans—are more interested in getting their way than getting something done. Being a <u>partisan</u>—a supporter of one's party—is more important than doing what one was elected to do.

persecute—*v.* to oppress. The Nazis <u>persecuted</u> Jews in World War II. The Romans <u>persecuted</u> Christians for hundreds of years. European colonists <u>persecuted</u> Native Americans for hundreds of years. Unfortunately, the history of mankind is filled with <u>persecution</u>.

petition—*n.* a formal request to a government or another authority. You have probably signed a <u>petition</u> at some point in your life. Last year I signed a <u>petition</u> to end the dress code at my school, but it didn't work—we still have a dress code!

pivotal—*adj.* the most important. The <u>pivotal</u> moment of my last baseball game was when the other team had the bases loaded and I struck out their best hitter. That's what I call <u>pivotal</u>.

polarize—*v.* to cause two groups to focus on their differences. The issue of slavery <u>polarized</u> the United States in the 1800s.

pragmatist—*n.* someone who is practical. A <u>pragmatist</u> tends to support things he thinks can actually be done. For example, a <u>pragmatist</u> would be satisfied if a last-place team just improved a little, and maybe the next year made it to the middle of the pack. He wouldn't expect the team to go from last place to first place in one year, because that wouldn't be practical.

preservation—*n.* protection from destruction. This word is used most often when people are talking about <u>preserving</u> old buildings in their town (historic <u>preservation</u>) and when people are talking about <u>preserving</u> the environment (environmental <u>preservation</u>).

primary source—*n.* a first-hand record of an event. I was doing a report on how the Magic's Tracy McGrady got so good. Some of my <u>primary sources</u> were videotapes of three high school games he played right before he got drafted and a scouting report the Magic did on him at a McDonald's All-Stars game.

productive—*adj.* able to produce a lot of stuff. A <u>productive</u> writer writes a lot of books and articles. A <u>productive</u> farmer harvests a lot of crops. A <u>productive</u> hitter hits a lot of extra-base hits and gets a lot of RBIs.

profit—*n.* in business, the money left over after you subtract the costs of making something that you sell. If it costs a company $20 to make a CD player and they sell it for $50, their <u>profit</u> is $30.

prohibit—*v.* to not allow; to forbid. Laws are basically created to <u>prohibit</u> bad behavior like drunk driving and stealing.

prosperity—*n.* success and riches. America is known for being a land of <u>prosperity</u>—there are a lot of people in this country who are rich and middle class. Many countries have no <u>prosperity</u> at

WhizTip

To remember pivotal, think about "pivot" which means "to turn."

Antonym

idealist—**n.** a person who wants the best things possible to happen, no matter how impractical those things may be.

Related Word

self-preservation— n. the act of doing things that help you survive.

Whiz Fact

Shakespeare was a very productive writer, writing around 40 plays and hundreds of poems in his lifetime.

Related Word

prosperous— adj. rich.

● all—everyone is poor.

● **provoke**—*v.* to anger; to egg on. Many animals are quite peaceful until they are provoked. Most bears won't even pay you any attention, but if you provoke them by poking them with a stick or shooting at them, you are in big trouble.

● **purchasing power**—*n.* the ability of people to buy things. A person's purchasing power is affected by how much money he makes.

● **public domain**—*n.* land that's owned by the state or government instead of by a person. Theoretically, that means all taxpayers "own" and can use the land. In the West, a lot of livestock graze on land that's public domain.

● **quarantine**—*n.* enforced isolation. When my family spent a month in England, we brought our dog with us. Joe had to be quarantined for the first week in England to make sure she didn't have any diseases. Joe was not pleased.

● **radical**—*n.* someone who works for political or social revolution. Our country has a complicated relationship with radicals. When we were colonies breaking from England, we were the radicals, breaking the law. Now, as the most powerful nation in the world, we generally look down on radicals. And as a country based on the rule of law, revolution is not really our cup of tea. Just look at the famous radicals our country has had to see how complicated our relationship with them is.

● **ratify**—*v.* to pass. After a law is written, it has to be ratified by both houses of Congress—the House of Representatives and the Senate, before it is signed (or vetoed) by the president.

● **ration**—*v.* to give out in restricted amounts, usually during wartime, to conserve resources. Food and fuel are often rationed during wartime so more resources can be devoted to fighting the battles.

● **rebellion**—*n.* a revolt against authority. Have you noticed how many words there are in this section that basically mean "revolt" and "rebel"? It is an important subject when it comes to the history of our country. Rebellion was involved when the colonies broke from England. Rebels also have qualities that we as Americans value in a person—they go out on their own, no matter what anyone thinks.

● **Reconstruction**—*n.* the period after the Civil War when the South was controlled by the federal government, before those states were readmitted to the Union (1865-1877).

● **recruit**—*v.* to get someone to join something. The most obvious use for this word is when people are talking about recruiting sol-

---

DOUBLE MEANING

public domain—n. books, articles, and products that aren't protected by a copyright. (Note: This book is NOT public domain!)

Whiz Fact

Famous radicals include crazy writer Abbie Hoffman, presidential assassin Lee Harvey Oswald, and President Thomas Jefferson, who was a big fan of revolutions.

DOUBLE MEANING

ration—n. quantities of food.

Whiz Tip

To remember Reconstruction, think of "reconstructing"— or rebuilding— the country.

diers to join the armed forces. But people are also <u>recruited</u> to join the soccer team, the PTA, and to attend a particular college.

reform—*v.* to change for the better. One of the great things about our government is that if a law—or the government—doesn't work, we can <u>reform</u> it by voting for representatives who want <u>reform</u>.

regional—*adj.* area-specific. My baseball team plays in a <u>regional</u> tournament every year—that's the tournament where all the teams from the Miami-Ft. Lauderdale <u>region</u> play.

regulate—*v.* to control. The government <u>regulates</u> all kinds of things. The most important may be the toxic emissions from cars and power plants. The government <u>regulates</u> the poisons in those emissions by setting limits the companies must not exceed. If the company doesn't follow those <u>regulations</u>, the company gets fined.

repeal—*v.* to take back; to rescind. Sometimes a law is <u>repealed</u> because is was really a bad, bad idea. One of the reasons the colonies broke from England was that England wouldn't <u>repeal</u> tax laws that were really hard on the colonies.

representation—*n.* the act of <u>representing</u> something or someone. In the phrase "taxation without <u>representation</u>," it means not having <u>representatives</u> in the government looking after your interests. The main reason the colonies broke with England was that they were being taxed, but had no say at all in how much they were taxed and why.

republic—*n.* a government where the people elect representatives to do their bidding. The United States is a <u>republic</u>.

resolute—*adj.* firm; unwavering. I am <u>resolute</u> in my view that the Orlando Magic are the best team in basketball, no matter what their actual record is.

retaliation—*n.* the act of striking back after you get attacked. It is not good to start a fight, but sometimes you have to <u>retaliate</u>. Lincoln issued the Order of Retaliation in 1863 saying that if the South violated the rules of war by killing or enslaving captured Union soldiers, the Union would <u>retaliate</u> by doing the same to their soldiers.

revenue—*n.* money made. Government gets its <u>revenue</u> from taxes. Companies get their <u>revenue</u> by selling things. I get my <u>revenue</u> from my allowance and mowing lawns.

sanctuary—*n.* protection from arrest or deportation. People who flee persecution in their countries are often given <u>sanctuary</u> in the United States.

secede—*v.* to break away from a unit. The South <u>seceded</u> from the

List three regulations at your school:

1. _____
2. _____
3. _____

surrender—**v.** to give up.

DOUBLE MEANING
sanctuary—**n.** a natural area where plants and animals are protected is called a wildlife sanctuary (science).

United States in 1861. That's what started the Civil War, because President Lincoln would not let them do it without a fight. The South's <u>secession</u> was a pivotal moment in this country's history.

secondary source—*n.* a summary or an account of an event or person. When I wrote my report on Tracy McGrady, secondary sources I used included two *Sports Illustrated* articles on him and the biography they have on him at *www.nba.com*.

segregation—*n.* the separation of people who are different. Blacks were <u>segregated</u> from white society for years in this country. In some churches, women and men are <u>segregated</u>, with women sitting on one side, men on the other. Boys are often <u>segregated</u> from girls in gym class. <u>Segregation</u> keeps people apart.

serf—*n.* a member of the lowest class in feudal Europe. <u>Serfs</u> basically worked the lords' lands and got some gruel in return.

siege—*n.* in war, a sustained attack. In World War I, troops were under a continuous state of <u>siege</u>. The fighting never stopped as the soldiers on both sides dug trenches and refused to give an inch.

sovereign—*n.* a king or queen. We don't have any sovereigns in our country. England still has its <u>sovereigns</u>, but they don't have any power anymore. They are just symbols of England's past.

stereotype—*n.* a judgment based on oversimple assumptions. You are using a <u>stereotype</u> when you think a person or group of people are a certain way for no real reason. *Example*: Italian Americans are often <u>stereotyped</u> as being in the Mafia. Blonde women are often <u>stereotyped</u> as being ditzy. Obviously, a <u>stereotype</u> has nothing to do with an individual person. It's just a lazy way to form opinions of people.

To remember subversive means "undermining" remember sub means "under."

subversive—*adj.* undermining. As part of preparing for a war against France, Thomas Jefferson signed the Alien and Sedition Acts, which outlawed <u>subversive</u> behavior like criticizing the government. Now we can criticize the government as much as we want.

To remember suffrage, remember people "suffer" when they don't have the right to vote.

suffrage—*n.* the right to vote. Women gained <u>suffrage</u> in this country in 1920. Eighteen-year-olds gained <u>suffrage</u> after the Vietnam War when they argued that, if they could go to war, why couldn't they vote?

sympathizers—*n.* people who agree with something and want to help; people who are <u>sympathetic</u> to a person or a cause. Usually in American history, the word is used in the term "communist <u>sympathizers</u>," which means people who agreed with the communists and helped them out in the early 20th century.

tariffs—*n.* taxes on imports and exports. High <u>tariffs</u> on the colonies' imports and exports made colonists mad at England. You know what happened next.

temperance—*n.* the policy of not drinking alcohol. There was a <u>temperance</u> movement in the United States in the early 20th century that made drinking alcohol illegal. That was when gangsters like Al Capone made millions selling illegal booze.

transcend—*v.* to surpass; to overcome. Sometimes you have to <u>transcend</u> your limitations to reach your goals. If your vocabulary is a limitation for you, this book should help you <u>transcend</u> that obstacle.

Treasury—*n.* the part of the government in charge of the money supply. Our <u>Treasury</u> Department makes sure there is enough, but not too much, money floating around to keep the economy moving.

truce—*n.* a stop in the fighting. Sometimes in a war the sides just call a <u>truce</u> without anyone declaring victory. They just stop fighting because they are tired of seeing their people killed.

unanimous—*adj.* being in complete agreement. In a <u>unanimous</u> decision, everyone votes the same way. When we took a vote from the students at school about our dress code, the students voted <u>unanimously</u> to repeal it.

urban—*adj.* related to the city. Lots of big cities around the country have been undergoing <u>urban</u> renewal, which means they are working to improve the quality of their inner cities and downtown areas.

usurp—*v.* to take over; to seize power. Many times members of Congress have tried to <u>usurp</u> the authority of the president by passing legislation that lessens the president's power. Sometimes they have prevailed, sometimes they have failed.

utopia—*n.* a perfect world. Many systems of government promise their followers a <u>utopia</u> on Earth. I think Key West is the closest anyone has come to <u>utopia</u> yet!

verdict—*n.* a decision in a court case. It is the job of a jury to reach a <u>verdict</u> in a case. When members of a jury don't reach a verdict, it's called a "hung jury."

veto—*n.* rejection of a proposal. In our government, a <u>veto</u> is a president's vote against legislation passed by Congress. Presidents often <u>veto</u> legislation they don't agree with.

viable—*adj.* possible. A "<u>viable</u> option" is an option that could work. However, in my quest to get my sister Jenny to switch her bedroom with me, I offered her many options I thought were <u>viable</u>. But none of them ended up working. So I am stuck in my

Whiz Quiz
Name a limitation you have had to transcend in your life:
_____
_____
_____

Related Word
majority—adj. In a majority vote, more than 50 percent of the people vote one way, but not everybody.

Antonym
rural—adj. related to the countryside.

Whiz Tip
Fruitopia is a fruit drink that plays off the word utopia: Fruitopia is supposed to be the "perfect" fruit drink.

little closet-sized room, while she lives in luxury.

mandatory—adj. forced.

voluntary—*adj.* of one's own choice, with no outside force. Our armed forces are now <u>voluntary</u>, but in times of war, you can be forced to fight. At my school, joining band or sports is <u>voluntary</u>, but everyone must take math and science.

WhizWords

communism
democracy
despotism
fascism
federalism
imperialism
republic

Social Studies

Government

I was over at my great-grandfather's assisted living complex the other day, and he was going on and on about World War II. He's a good guy, but when you get him started on World War II, you might as well pull up a chair because you're going to be there for a while. Anyway, he was talking about **fascism** and **communism** and all of these different kinds of governments I have only heard of in Social Studies class.

It made me realize that I wrongly assumed that all countries are **democracies** like ours. When my great-grandfather was growing up, Germany had a **fascist** government; Russia was part of the Soviet Union and was a **communist** country; **imperialism** was the favorite kind of government for all kinds of kings in the Middle East; and the African countries that weren't run as colonies by France and England were run by **despots.**

My great-grandfather lived in crazy times! Today, the Middle East oil countries are still pretty much all run by kings, and Africa is still full of **despots,** but lots of the rest of the countries—like Germany and Japan— have gone **democratic.**

Related Word

nationalism—n. Nationalism is a bad thing when it means you really like your country, but hate all the other countries. Nazi Germany was based on intense nationalism. The Nazis were going to rule the whole world, and kill anyone they thought was unworthy of being a member of the Third Reich.

IDENTIFY THE GOVERNMENT TYPE EXERCISE

Following are some countries that have gone through some big changes over the years. If you don't know what kind of government was in place on the dates I give you (and from the hints in my descriptions), do some research in the library or on the Internet to find out. You will be very surprised by what you find.

Country	Year	Government?
England	1714	King George I assumes the throne.
Texas	1836	Texas is an independent republic.
United States	1897	William McKinley is elected our 25th president.
Germany	1935	Hitler rules with an iron fist.
Jordan	1953	King Hussein assumes his hereditary position.
Cambodia	1976	The totalitarian Khmer Rouge wreak havoc.
England	1979	Margaret Thatcher is elected the first woman prime minister.

Whenever you hear about a country in the news that you don't know anything about, do some research and figure out what kind of government it has. I've been doing this for the last few months whenever I hear about a country in Africa and Asia, because I don't know very much about those two continents. It is really scary how few democracies there are out there!

WhizWords

agitator
anarchy
insurgent
insurrection
militant
radical
rebellion
subversive

Social Studies
Revolution

Related Word

utopia—n.
a perfect world.
Many rebellions
are led by
agitators who
promise their
followers utopia.

Rebellion is a tricky subject. Whether a revolution is good or bad often depends on what side you are on. For example, the colonists' **rebellion** against mother England is the only reason the United States of America even exists. And our democracy was a big experiment at the time. The fact that it worked basically opened the door for democracies everywhere. So there—a "good" **insurrection.**

But if you watch the news every day, you see **revolutions** all over the place, and they are not pretty, and the result of the **rebellion** is not always good.

THREE HISTORIES OF REBELLION EXERCISE

From our history and the continuing events in many countries, you can see why words about rebellion and revolution are so important to know. To get a better handle on the vocabulary often used to describe revolution and revolutionaries, I want you to write one short essay comparing and contrasting any two rebellions. For your convenience, I'll go ahead and list some of the more interesting rebellions of the past few hundred years:

1. 1776: Colonists rebel against England
2. 1789: The French rebel against King Louis XVI
3. 1917: Russians rebel against the czar
4. 1956: Communists in Cuba revolt

Be sure to use all of the "Revolution" words in the essay, and try to squeeze in the Related Words as well. If, when you have completed your exercise, you want to make sure you are comfortable with the words, compare two of the remaining rebellions to test yourself.

Related Word

sympathizer—n.
a person who
agrees with a
cause and wants
to help. A
sympathizer
might participate
in subversive
activities to
support a
radical cause.

Social Studies

Inequality

WhizWords
abolitionist
bias
discriminate
emancipation
feminism
integration
intolerant
oppress
persecute
segregation
stereotype
suffrage

People rebel because they feel they are being **oppressed** or **discriminated** against. **Feminists** fight for the rights of women every day because women don't have the same rights as men. **Abolitionists** fought for the freedom of slaves, who didn't have any rights at all. In fact, the history of our country is filled with situations where individuals had to overcome **bias**. It was once common to **discriminate** based on race and gender. And our country is called the land of the free! So you can just imagine what life is like in countries where equality isn't even considered important.

Luckily in the United States, we have made great strides. There is pretty much universal **suffrage** now—everyone over the age of 18 can vote. Our public schools, public places, and the military are all **integrated**, too. **Segregation** used to keep white people and black people apart.

Even so, there is still a lot of **intolerance** around. Lots of the advances in equality have happened in the past 20 or 30 years, but old habits die hard. So some people still use **stereotypes** to judge those who are different than they are.

Related Word

diversity—n.
variety.
Diversity and
integration can
help people
learn that
stereotypes
and biases
are shallow
and stupid.

SUFFRAGE FOR FASHION MODELS EXERCISE

The fight for equal rights is a serious business. People have given their lives so that others might have equal opportunity. However, for this exercise, let's lighten things up a little. Pretend there is only one group left in this country that is being discriminated against: skinny fashion models. Now, get a pencil and paper and write a make-believe history about how skinny fashion models go from being segregated, discriminated against, and not having the right to vote, to being integrated, having equal rights, and having suffrage in the year 2050. Use as many of the words above as you can.

ESSAY

**The History of Skinny Fashion Models' Fight
For Suffrage in the 21st Century**

WhizWords

ambition
carpetbagger
civic
impeachment
inaugurate
lame duck
mandate
partisan

Social Studies
Politics

WhizTip

The best way to build your vocabulary is to read, read, and read some more. Newspapers are a good source of reading material. You'll find new information about things you're interested in every day.

Did you pay attention to the 2000 presidential race? When it started I didn't pay too much attention. But my dad is such a big Bush fan, he made me go to some rallies, and I started to get excited. And then the election! Nobody won! It took them about a month to figure out who the next president was going to be. It was the first time I stopped thinking about golf and started thinking about something else outside of school.

The election got me started reading the political stories in the newspaper. That's when I started to realize there were a ton of words I didn't know very well. For example—**carpetbagger.** Have you ever heard that word? And **lame duck.** I mean, what do ducks have to do with politics, especially ducks that waddle with a limp?

Apparently a lot, because **lame duck** and **carpetbagger** kept coming up over and over again, along with **impeachment, mandate,** and **partisan.** It's no wonder they are important to know for the FCAT and other tests. If you know these words, you will be a more informed citizen, and, therefore, probably vote for the right person more often. At least that's the idea.

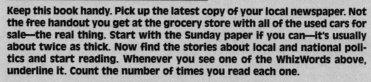

READ THE POLITICS PAGE EXERCISE

Keep this book handy. Pick up the latest copy of your local newspaper. Not the free handout you get at the grocery store with all of the used cars for sale—the real thing. Start with the Sunday paper if you can—it's usually about twice as thick. Now find the stories about local and national politics and start reading. Whenever you see one of the WhizWords above, underline it. Count the number of times you read each one.

Keep doing this for one week. That's right—read the political stories every day for one week. People may think you are crazy, but do it anyway. You can still read the sports page and the comics (my personal favorites), but read political news first. Underline, count, write the totals down below.

	Day 1	Day 2	Day 3	Day 4	Day 5	Day 6	Day 7
ambition							
carpetbagger							
civic							
impeachment							
inaugurate							
lame duck							
mandate							
partisan							

Which word won? Which came in second? Make sure you know the top three like the back of your hand, and make sure you know the rest of them like the front of your hand.

WhizWords

boom and bust
capitalism
commerce
commodity
economy
entrepreneur
free enterprise
profit
purchasing power

Social Studies

Economics

Did I say this country was all about freedom and equality? Just ask Alex Rodriguez, who signed a contract with the Texas Rangers for over $250 million, what this country is all about. Show me the money!

I mean, I love Alex Rodriguez. He is definitely the best shortstop in the league. But $250 million? I think he gets like $50,000 for each at bat or something like that. I only get $10/week for my allowance! Maybe Alex can spare a few hundred bucks?

No wonder tests ask so many questions about the U.S. **economy** and our **free enterprise** system. As a citizen of the richest country on the planet, it is important that you know how **capitalism** works so you can carry on the tradition. Especially if you end up being Alex Rodriguez!

READ THE BUSINESS PAGE EXERCISE

This exercise is basically a repeat of the politics exercise. After you get done with your week of reading the political stories in the paper, I want you to do a week of reading the business stories in the paper. I know—and you thought it couldn't get any more boring than politics!

Here's your chart for the week:

	Day 1	Day 2	Day 3	Day 4	Day 5	Day 6	Day 7
boom and bust							
capital							
capitalize							
commerce							
commodity							
economy							
entrepreneur							
free enterprise							
profit							

Again, know the Top Three like the back of your hand and the rest like the front of your hand.

Chapter 3

Math

absolute value—*n.* the distance from a point on a number line to zero; the numerical value of a quantity, regardless of its sign. Example: |5| = 5 and |–5| = 5.

On the FCAT

Which angle must the soccer player take to get to the goalpost?

angle—*n.* the figure formed when two lines meet at a point. There are three kinds of <u>angles</u>: acute (less than 90°), obtuse (greater than 90°), and right (90°).

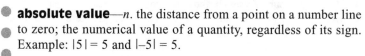

acute angle   obtuse angle   right angle

angle—*n.* oh yeah, there are two more kinds of angles—complementary and supplementary. <u>Complementary angles</u> add up to 90°. <u>Supplementary angles</u> add up to 180°.

On the FCAT

What is the area of the floor in square feet?

area—*n.* the amount of surface on a figure. For example, a rectangle's <u>area</u> is length x width. A triangle's <u>area</u> is 1/2 base x height. A circle's <u>area</u> is πr^2. Just remember: <u>area</u> is the amount of space inside the lines.

DOUBLE MEANING
average—n.
nothing special,
middle-of-the-road,
normal.

average—*n.* what you get when you add up a bunch of numbers and then divide by the number of numbers you added up. The <u>average</u> of the numbers 9, 13, 28, 72, 83 = (9 + 13 + 28 + 72 + 83) ÷ 5 = 205 ÷ 5 = 41. So 41 is the <u>average</u> of those 5 numbers.

bisect—*v.* to divide into two usually equal parts. In math, a line or a point usually <u>bisects</u> another line. It cuts that line in two. Once in science we had to dissect a frog, and I had to <u>bisect</u> its brain—I actually cut its brain in half. I almost fainted.

capacity—*n.* the amount something can hold. *Example*: My dad's Nissan Stanza's gas tank has a <u>capacity</u> of 12 gallons of gas.

circumference—*n.* the length of the boundary of a circle. If you took a circle and straightened out the line that surrounds it and measured it, that's its <u>circumference</u>. The formula to find a circle's circumference is $2\pi r$, with *r* standing for radius.

congruent—*adj.* having the same shape and size. If you put one <u>congruent</u> shape on top of the other, they would be exactly the same.

In math, this is most often used to describe <u>congruent</u> triangles.

consecutive—*adj.* occurring in order, one right after the other. In math, it is most often used to describe <u>consecutive</u> numbers in a number pattern. Players also talk about how hard it is to play on <u>consecutive</u> days in sports like baseball and basketball because they don't get to rest between games.

convert—*v.* to change from one system of measurement to another, most often used when <u>converting</u> our system of measurements to the metric system. See the metrics page at the end of this section for some common measurements and <u>conversions</u>.

converge—*v.* to come together at a point. Lines <u>converge</u>. So do rivers. In Pennsylvania, the Allegheny and Monongahela rivers <u>converge</u> to form the Ohio River.

coordinates—*n.* a set of two numbers that shows where a point goes on a <u>coordinate</u> plane. So what is a <u>coordinate plane</u>, you ask? It is that t-shaped thingie . . . oh just look over in the margin.

denominator—*n.* the number under the line in a fraction.

diagonal—*n.* in a rectangle, a line slanting from one corner to the other. The "Diver Down" flag used by scuba divers has a <u>diagonal</u> line across it—that's a good way to get a visual of the word <u>diagonal</u>.

diameter—*n.* the length across the middle of a circle. If you are given the radius of the circle, double it to get the <u>diameter</u>: $d = 2r$.

digit—*n.* 1, 2, 3, 4, 5, 6, 7, 8, 9, 0 are digits. Math problems are always using 2-<u>digit</u> numbers (also called tens: 23, 61), 3-<u>digit</u> numbers (also called hundreds: 154, 982), and 4-<u>digit</u> numbers (also called thousands:1,468).

dividend—*n.* a number divided by another number. In the math problem 64 ÷ 6, 64 is the <u>dividend</u> (6 is the divisor).

divisor—*n.* the number that divides another number. See *dividend*.

exponent—*n.* a number off to the upper right of another number that shows the power to which the number is raised. That means whatever the <u>exponent</u> is, you multiply a number times itself that many times. $4^3 = 4 \times 4 \times 4 = 64$.

factor—*n.* a number that can be multiplied with others to achieve a product. Hmm. How can I put this. Pick a number. The numbers you multiply to get that number are its <u>factors</u>. Take the number 27 for instance: its <u>factors</u> are 3 x 3 x 3 (= 27); 9 x 3 (=27); and 27 x 1 (=27). The number 13's <u>factors</u> are 13 x 1 (= 13). Note: 13 is also a prime number—which means its only <u>factors</u> are itself and 1.

Bar Graph

graphs—*n.* you need to know how to read two main kinds of graphs—<u>circle graphs</u> and <u>bar graphs</u>. A <u>circle graph</u> is also called a <u>pie graph</u>. The different sized slices of pie show relative proportions of something, like the amount of attention four brothers and sisters get from their parents. A <u>bar graph</u> measures things on an *x* and *y* axis. The *x* axis stands for one thing (like years) and the *y* axis stands for another (like height). *Note*: You may also see <u>line graphs</u> here and there: they look like a jagged mountain top set on an *x* axis.

**Circle Graph
(Pie Graph)**

horizontal—*adj.* straight across. To remember this word, think of the *horizon*.

hypotenuse—*n.* the longest side of a right triangle; the side opposite the 90° angle. About the only time you will see questions about the <u>hypotenuse</u> is in questions about right triangles.

Whiz Quiz

Circle the integers.
1/2
.6
6
–6
–2
0
3.2
6.9
3/4
17
–12
243

integers—*n.* positive whole numbers, negative whole numbers, and zero are integers. No fractions and no decimals are <u>integers</u>—ever! Think of <u>integers</u> as having too much "integrity" to get involved with messy fractions and decimals.

intersect—*v.* to cross each other. Lines <u>intersect</u> on graphs. To remember it, think of street <u>intersections</u>—where streets cross each other.

irrational number—*n.* a number that cannot be expressed as a fraction or decimal. Like π, or $\sqrt{2}$. You can put an <u>irrational number</u> on a number line, but you can't express the number precisely, like you can with 1.5 and –3. (See the definition for *rational number* if you don't get it yet.)

mean—*n.* see the definition for *average* (they are the same thing).

median—*n.* in a group of numbers, it is the one in the middle or the average of the two numbers in the middle. *Example*: Here is a group of numbers: 23, 31, 67, 78, 86, 165, 254. The <u>median</u> is 78—it is the middle number in this series.

On the FCAT

In January, on how many days was the snowfall greater than the daily mean snowfall?

metric—*adj.* related to the measuring system based on tens. (See *Measurements* on page 53.)

mode—*n.* in a group of numbers, it is the number that occurs most often. *Example*: Here is a group of numbers: 23, 24, 24, 25, 26, 27, 28, 29, 29, 30, 31, 32, 32, 32, 33, 34. The mode is 32. It occurs three times—the most of any number in this series.

multiple—*n.* a number that you can divide another number into and get zero remainder. 4, 8, and 12 are multiples of 2.

negative number—*n.* a number less than zero indicated by a minus sign (–). On a number line, the numbers to the left of 0 are negative numbers.

numerator—*n.* the number on top of the line in a fraction.

ordered pair—*n.* the actual coordinates on a coordinate plane (x,y). (See the definition for *coordinates*.)

parallel—*adj.* relating to lines traveling alongside each other at the same distance without ever touching. Train tracks are parallel.

perimeter—*n.* the outside edge of an object or shape. Think about soldiers patrolling the perimeter of their outpost. That means they are patrolling the edges of their camp, making sure the enemy isn't planning any funny business.

perpendicular—*adj.* relating to lines meeting each other at a right (90°) angle. Perpendicular is kind of the opposite of *parallel*. They are mentioned in the same sentence—and the same math problem—all the time.

perspective—*n.* the appearance of depth or three dimensions. Think about drawing a road that recedes into the distance— the sides of the road get closer together as they go away into the distance. Oh heck, sometimes a picture is worth a thousand words, so just look at the picture of the road on the left. That's perspective.

point—*n.* in geometry, a spot marked in space. Basically, a point is used in questions about "the distance between two points" and "the straight line between points A and B." Stuff like that. The points are the dots.

polygon—*n.* a flat shape with three or more straight sides. A polygon is any shape with flat sides, really, from a triangle to a rectangle to an octagon to whatever a shape with 28 sides is called, and beyond . . . .

positive number—*n.* a number greater than zero. On a number line, the numbers to the right of 0 are positive numbers.

prime number—*n.* a positive, whole number with only itself and one as factors. That means you can't divide any other number into it without getting a remainder. 17 is a prime number. 23 is a prime number. Try all night, you can't divide any other numbers into prime numbers without getting a remainder. (See the definition for *factor* for more information.)

probability—*n.* a number used to describe the chance that

$$\frac{3}{5} \xleftarrow{\text{numerator}}$$

On the FCAT

Which ordered pair represents point *c* on the graph?

perspective

Antonym

negative number— **n. a number less than zero. The numbers to the left of 0 on a number line.**

49

Math

On the FCAT

What is the
probability that
Maria will get the
blue shoes?

On the FCAT

How would the
product 5 x 5 x 5
be expressed in
exponential
notation?

Related Word

random sample—n.
a group of
numbers or
values chosen
out of the blue.

On the FCAT

If the triangle
were reflected
over the
y-axis, what would
its new coordi-
nates be?

something will happen. *Example*: When you flip a coin, the probability that the coin will come up heads is 1/2, since there are two equally possible outcomes.

product—*n.* the answer of a multiplication problem. The product of 3 x 6 is 18.

proportion—*n.* an equation showing two ratios are equal. *Example*: 2/6 = 1/3.

Pythagorean theorem—*n.* for right triangles, the sum of the squares of a right triangle's sides is equal to the square of the hypotenuse. $a^2 + b^2 = hyp^2$. (See the definitions for *hypotenuse* and *triangle* for more information.)

quadrilateral—*n.* a four-sided polygon. Squares, rectangles, and rhombuses are all quadrilaterals.

radius—*n.* the line from the center of a circle to its outside edge. The radius is half a circle's diameter.

random—*adj.* having no pattern or reason; out of the blue. Lottery numbers are randomly chosen by that ping pong ball machine.

ratio—*n.* the relationship between two quantities, pretty much the same as *proportion* (see definition above). The ratio of 4 to 9 is written 4/9; the ratio of 6 to 7 is written 6/7.

rational number—*n.* a number that can be expressed as a ratio of two integers. 7 is a rational number because it can be written as 7/1. −2/3 is a rational number. 45.4 is a rational number.

reflection—*n.* a shape that is flipped, so it's the same, but backwards. Think of it like your reflection in the mirror. All the sides are the same length and the angles are the same size, they are just positioned exactly opposite of where they were.

rotation—*n.* movement in a circular motion around a fixed point. When a geometric shape is rotated, its shape stays the same but the side that was on the bottom may now be on the top.

scale—*n.* when talking about models, scale is the relationship between the size of the model and the size of the real-life object. So if a scale model of an airplane is 1:8, that means the real airplane is 8 times as big as the model.

scientific notation—*n.* writing a number in terms of its powers of ten. For example, 3,414 is 3.414×10^3.

square—*n.* the number you get when you multiply a number by itself. The square of 3 (also written as 3^2) is 9. The square of 11 (or 11^2) = 121.

square root—*n.* the divisor of a number that when multiplied by itself gives that number. So 6 is the square root of 36 because 6^2 is 36. The symbol for square root is $\sqrt{\ }$, so the square root of 36 can be written as $\sqrt{36}$.

symmetry—*n.* when the stuff on one side of a dividing line matches the stuff on the other; a balanced arrangement. If you draw a line down the middle of your face, the parts on the left match the parts on the right. Your face has <u>symmetry</u>. It is <u>symmetrical</u>. So are some shapes and some graphs.

tessellation *n.*—a repeating pattern of congruent figures that completely covers a plane, with no interruptions.

three-dimensional—*adj.* having three dimensions, which gives an object depth. Any real object is <u>three-dimensional</u>. Also written as <u>3-D</u>.

triangle—*n.* a shape with three sides and three angles. There are four main kinds of <u>triangles</u> you need to know:

On the FCAT
How must you move the drawing to make a symmetrical cookie?

On the FCAT
The squares form the tessellated pattern shown in Diagram B.

equilateral   All sides and angles are equal.

isosceles   Two sides and their opposite angles are equal.

right   One angle is 90°. The side opposite the 90° angle is the hypotenuse.

scalene   All sides and angles are different from each other.

two-dimensional—*adj.* having two dimensions, which means the object has no depth (it resides on a single plane). Also written as <u>2-D</u>.

unit cost—*n.* the cost of each single thing. <u>Unit cost</u> is usually used in problems where you have to find out how much it costs to make something: *Example*: What is the unit cost of gum if you can make 50,000 pieces of gum for $725. Answer: $.0145 per piece of gum. (Divide $725 by 50,000). Then they have you compare that <u>unit cost</u> to another one, so you can see which manufacturing method is cheapest! (Watch out. You are being trained.)

variable—*n.* a symbol whose value can change. In math, the

Math

Whiz Quiz

Solve the
following
problems with
the **variables**

$x=2$ and $y=3$

$2x$

$4y$

$-5y$

$x - y$

$2y + 7x$

$-2x - 4y$

On the FCAT

What is the
volume in cubic
units of this stack
of pennies?

variable is usually called x or y. That means you can plug in different numbers for the variable x or y or z or whatever. To remember the word, think of watching a weather report. The weatherman often says that "winds are variable," and weather itself is always variable (changing).

vertical—*adj.* going straight up and down. Like a flag pole.

volume—*n.* the amount of space something occupies. You can get Coca-Cola in all kinds of different volumes, from a 12-ounce can to a 16-ounce bottle to a 3-liter bottle. I prefer the 3-liter bottle.

Math
Measurements Page

METRIC AND BRITISH IMPERIAL MEASUREMENTS

Measurement conversions charts are provided on most math tests, so it's important for you to know how to read them. Measuring is the only time I wish I was European. They have things so easy when it comes to measuring. As you probably know, their metric system is all based on tens. Anyway, here are the measurements that are used most often on tests—in metric and British Imperial (that's what we use). Don't ask me why we use British Imperial and the English use metrics. Because I don't know.

BRITISH IMPERIAL

Distance

Foot	12 inches
Yard	3 feet
Mile	1,760 yards

Volume

Pint	16 ounces
Quart	2 pints
Gallon	4 quarts

Weight

Pound	16 ounces
Ton	2,000 pounds

METRIC

Distance

Centimeter	10 millimeters
Meter	100 centimeters
Kilometer	1,000 meters

Volume

Liter	1,000 milliliters

Weight

Gram	1,000 milligrams
Kilogram	1,000 grams
Metric ton	1,000 kilograms

COMMON CONVERSIONS
(ALL CONVERSIONS ARE APPROXIMATE)

Distance

BRITISH IMPERIAL	METRIC
Inch	about 3 centimeters
Yard	about 1 meter
Mile	about 1.6 kilometers

Volume

BRITISH IMPERIAL	METRIC
Ounce	about 29 milliliters
Cup	about 1/4 liter
Gallon	about 3.79 liters

Weight

BRITISH IMPERIAL	METRIC
Ounce	about 29 grams
Pound	about 450 grams (about 1/2 kilogram)

WhizWords

bar graph*
circle graph*
coordinates
line graph

*See definition
for <u>graph</u>.

Math

Graphs

So many people say—Why do I need to learn all this math? I'll never use it in real life. I think I'll spend my time shopping on eBay.

Well, nothing could be further from the truth. Lots of people use math every day. In baseball, they use math to calculate hitters' batting averages. Players can then use those batting averages to negotiate their salaries. Then, when they are buying their yachts and mansions, they use math to calculate sales tax and change. Even if you're not an All-Star baseball player, you'll still need to know math. How else are you going to budget to save up for those great deals on eBay?

Now that you are convinced, let's start with something relatively simple that is used all the time: a graph. There is nothing better for explaining things in an easy-to-read format than a chart or a graph

USING MATH TO EXPLAIN YOUR LIFE EXERCISE
You can use a graph to represent just about any relationship. I have created the following graphs to represent:

My math test grades last semester:
67, 92, 89, 94, 78, 81, 88, 97

The four TV shows I watch the most, in relative proportion to the amount of time spent viewing:

Digimon **10%**
Moesha **30%**
Buffy **20%**
Baseball **40%**

My height over the years:

Years	3	6	9	12
Feet	3	3.5	4	4.75

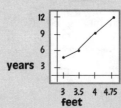

Now you draw the same three graphs for your most recent math grades, viewing time for your favorite TV shows, and your height at different ages. Try to think of three more things you can represent on a graph. Here are some ideas: raises or drops in your allowance in the last two years, the proportions of kinds of food you eat every day (circle), and the amount of time you spend daily on various activities like sleeping, eating, going to school, doing homework, e-mailing your friends, and so on.

Circles

So you need more proof that math is all around you? Fine. Let's talk about circles. Circles are obviously everywhere, from the portholes on a ship to the circles under your parents' eyes. The invention of the wheel, the hardest working circle of all time, was a big event, right up there with the invention of Pop Rocks and Napster.

Of course on math tests, you have to do a little more than just appreciate the importance of roundness. You have to be able to calculate **diameters** and **circumferences** of circles of all sizes.

DIFFERENT SIZE CIRCLES EXERCISE

I have given you a variety of circles below. I want you to find the and diameter of each. I'm even going to help you out a bit. Here are the equations for each:

Diameter = $2r$

Circumference = $2\pi r$

Note: Circles not drawn to scale.

Now, get a ruler. Go and find five more circles in your house and measure the radius—that's the length of a straight line drawn from the center to the circumference (it's also half the diameter). Use those measurements to find the diameter and the circumference of the circles you found. Don't know where to start? Try the kitchen, the home of circular housewares.

Note: π is the ratio of the circumference of a circle to its diameter. The actual number π is approximately 3.14159.

WhizWords

integer
irrational number
negative number
positive number
prime number
rational number

Math
Number Types

Still not convinced of math's importance in your everyday existence? I was like you once, before I saw the light. One part of math you can't dispute is that numbers are everywhere. We measure ingredients, tell time, and count the days until summer vacation.

What you probably don't do while you are counting the days to summer vacation is think about what kind of number you have in your head. The "31" in "31 days until summer vacation" is an integer, a positive number, a prime number, and a rational number. Those are the kinds of things you need to know for the FCAT and other tests. So let's review.

NUMBERS YOU SEE EVERY DAY EXERCISE

Label each of the numbers with all of the number types from above that match. If none match, write "none." I'll do the first couple so you get the idea.

17 years old   integer, positive number, prime number, rational number

–3 degrees   integer, negative number, rational number

$.79 Snickers bar   _____

.327 batting average   _____

2 1/2 weeks   _____

4 hours   _____

–12 under par   _____

$12.50 pepperoni pizza   _____

A drink coaster with a circumference of 6π (okay, I'm stretching here)   _____

Math
Number Relationships

Whether you believe that math affects your everyday life or not, you still have to take tests about it. One thing that shows up on all sorts of math tests, including the FCAT, is number relationships. Questions about number relationships usually involve long lists of numbers and ask you to figure out the mean, median, or mode. Sometimes all three.

Just remember:
- mean (means average)
- median (in the middle of the road)
- mode (sounds like most)

So let's get to it.

TEST GRADES EXERCISE
Find the mean (average), median, and mode of my grades last year on tests in English, math, science, and social studies.

		Mean	Median	Mode
Language Arts	56, 92, 87, 79, 95, 92, 99			
Math	78, 82, 91, 79, 78, 97, 93			
Science	94, 91, 99, 100, 89, 94, 94			
Social Studies	102, 84, 72, 67, 84, 94, 84			

Find the mean, median, and mode of these three baseball players' batting averages over their careers.

		Mean	Median	Mode
Paul O'Neill	.333, .256, .252, .276, .270, .256, .246, .311, .359, .300, .302, .324, .317, .285, .283			
Manny Ramirez	.269, .308, .309, .328, .294, .333, .351			
Alex Rodriguez	.232, .358, .300, .310, .285, .316			
Derek Jeter	.314, .291, .324, .349, .339			
Tony Gwynn	.289, .309, .351, .317, .329, .370, .313, .336, .309, .317, .317, .358, .394, .368, .353, .372, .321, .338, .323			

For more practice, line up your grades from last semester or last year and find the mean, median, and mode.

Chapter 4

Science

acclimatization—*n.* adaptation to changes in climates. It took a while for my pet snake to become <u>acclimatized</u> to his new aquarium. He didn't eat any mice for a week!

adhere—*v.* to stick to. Scotch tape <u>adheres</u> to paper quite well. It does not <u>adhere</u> to running water.

angstrom unit—*n.* one hundred-millionth of a centimeter. <u>Angstroms</u> are used to measure radiation wavelengths.

asteroids—*n.* a bunch of big rocks orbiting the sun, kind of like mini-planets. Most <u>asteroids</u> are in between the planets Mars and Jupiter. In sci-fi movies, space ships are always getting caught up in <u>asteroid</u> belts. Just remember, they are called "belts" because they are "wrapping around" the sun.

atom—*n.* the smallest unit of an element that has all the properties of that element. Everything in the world is made up of <u>atoms</u>. The <u>atom</u> bomb gets its power from the splitting of <u>atoms</u>—that's how much energy is stored up in this tiny little particle. It's kind of scary when you think about it.

axis—*n.* the center around which something rotates. <u>Axis</u> is usually used when talking about a planet (like the Earth) rotating on its <u>axis</u>.

bacteria—*n.* one-celled organisms. They are all around us, but you can't see them. My mom buys anti-<u>bacterial</u> soap because she thinks my sister and I are getting too many colds—she thinks it's because of all the <u>bacteria</u> on our hands.

barometer—*n.* an instrument that measures pressure. You have probably heard your local weatherperson mention <u>barometric</u> pressure, which is the pressure of our own atmosphere. That pressure shifts as different weather patterns move in and out of the area.

beneficial—*adj.* helpful; good. Learning the words in this book should prove to be <u>beneficial</u> to your grades. Hey, it can't hurt!

biotic—*adj.* of or pertaining to life. You can remember this word by thinking of <u>antibiotic</u>, which is supposed to *kill* whatever microorganisms are living inside your body.

biodiversity—*n.* the range of life in a given environment. Earth's <u>biodiversity</u> is in constant jeopardy as people and industries cover the planet, displacing and destroying native species.

To remember **beneficial**, think of people giving **benefits** for charitable causes. That's a good thing to do.

biosphere—*n.* the part of the Earth and its atmosphere where living things exist.

boiling point—*n.* the temperature at which a liquid turns to gas. Different liquids have different <u>boiling points</u>.

buoyant—*adj.* it floats! Ivory soap is <u>buoyant</u>, but Zest and Irish Spring sink like stones.

carbon—*n.* the element found in all living things. One of the ways scientists find the age of a fossil is to use <u>carbon</u> dating. That's when they measure how much carbon is left in a fossil and calculate how old that makes it.

carnivore—*n.* meat-eater. The most ferocious <u>carnivore</u> known to mice is the house cat.

catalyst—*n.* in science, a substance that speeds up a chemical reaction. Fire is a <u>catalyst</u> for turning water into evaporated water.

catastrophic—*adj.* tragic and awful, causing great pain and suffering. I hope Tiger Woods doesn't suffer any <u>catastrophic</u> injuries in his career. That could ruin his run at Jack Nicklaus' record.

categorize—*v.* to divide up into groups. When my dad does the laundry, he always <u>categorizes</u> the clothes into whites and colors. I, on the other hand, just throw everything in together.

celestial—*adj.* related to the stars and the universe. Planets and asteroids and suns and stuff are all called "<u>celestial</u> bodies."

centrifugal force—*n.* moving away from the center. When you swing a bucket of water around in a circle really fast, and the water doesn't fall out, that's <u>centrifugal force</u>.

chain reaction—*n.* a series of events in which one thing leads to another, which leads to another. I saw a <u>chain reaction</u> accident on the highway once when a semi jackknifed and all of the cars behind it ran into each other.

chemical energy—*n.* energy stored in chemical compounds. <u>Chemical energy</u> is usually released in a chemical reaction when <u>chemical energy</u> changes into heat, light, or electricity.

circulatory system—*n.* the organs that move blood around the body, including the heart, veins, arteries, and capillaries. Just think of the pipes and plumbing that circulate water in your house. They

Whiz Fact

A bunch of scientists built an entire ecosystem under a big plastic bubble. They called it Biosphere II.

DOUBLE MEANING

catalyst—**n.** someone who makes things happen. Usually used in history when talking about a movement or revolution. The feminist movement's leader, Gloria Steinem, was a catalyst for change for women in the 1960s.

Antonym

centripetal force—**n.** moving toward the center. What keeps the planets orbiting around the sun.

are your house's <u>circulatory system</u>.

collision—*n.* the slamming of one thing into another. When there is a <u>collision</u> between an opponent's bat and my best pitch, that is not good.

combustible—*adj.* flammable. My science teacher tells us when a material we are working on is especially <u>combustible</u>. When we are working with <u>combustible</u> materials, all Bunsen burners are turned off!

complement—*v.* to make complete. In science, the word is often used to describe how an organ's structure <u>complements</u> its function. The shape of your esophagus (throat) <u>complements</u> its function by being straight and slippery—so food slides down it easily.

component—*n.* a part of a system or machine. The <u>components</u> of my stereo are the receiver, the CD player, and the five-speaker surround sound system.

compost—*n.* decayed organic matter that is used as fertilizer. <u>Compost</u> is made of a mixture of dead plants, and maybe manure. It smells awful, but it makes my mom's tomatoes grow fast.

condensation point—*n.* the temperature at which a gas condenses into a liquid. Clouds formed over the Marlins' last home game when the air temperature reached the <u>condensation point</u>. Clouds form when liquid collects on dust particles in the air.

conductor—*n.* a material that takes an electric current from one point to another. Copper wire is a good <u>conductor</u>. So are you, so stay away from electricity!

conservation—*n.* the protection of natural resources. <u>Conservation</u> is important if we are to keep the few natural wonders this country has left, like the Grand Canyon and Yellowstone National Park.

consistency—*n.* the degree of firmness or viscosity of a substance. A tub of margarine has a <u>consistency</u> similar to soft ice cream. The <u>consistency</u> of motor oil depends on the temperature—it gets really thick and gooey as the temperature drops.

constraint—*n.* something that limits or holds back something else. *Example:* The Hoover Dam acts as a <u>constraint</u> upon a rushing river.

contaminate—*v.* to make impure. Lots of things we do every day <u>contaminate</u> the environment. Driving a car <u>contaminates</u> the environment with carbon monoxide and other gases. Eating fast food <u>contaminates</u> the environment with all of the packaging it comes in, not to mention the pollution from the factories that make the packaging. It's almost like if you don't live in an underground house fueled by solar panels and windmills, you are <u>contaminating</u> the environment! About all we can do is try to reduce the amount of <u>contaminants</u> we produce, but we can never eliminate them.

continental drift—*n.* the theory that the continents are always drifting—they are not fixed. The continents drift only an average of .8 inches per year, but over thousands and millions of years, those few inches turn into miles.

WhizTip

Think of a train conductor getting you from one point to the next.

DOUBLE MEANING

consistent—adj. able to be counted on to behave the same way or produce the same thing all the time.

current—*n*. the flow of electricity.

cyclical—*adj*. happening in cycles. In chemistry, the word <u>cyclical</u> has to do with chemical compounds that have atoms arranged in a closed chain. In real life, lots of things are <u>cyclical</u>. The changing of seasons is the most obvious.

cytoplasm—*n*. the protoplasm outside the cell's nucleus.

decay—*v*. to rot; to break down. When you die, unless you have yourself cryogenically frozen or you are cremated, your body will <u>decay</u>. I plan on going the cryogenically frozen route, like in the original *Austin Powers* movie. Groovy baby, yeah!

decompose—*v*. to rot; to break down. (See *decay* above.) *Note*: <u>Decomposition</u> is also a *chemical reaction*.

dehydrate—*v*. to remove the water from. <u>Dehydrated</u> food like beef jerky has had the water taken out—that's why it's all shriveled. A few games ago I got <u>dehydrated</u> and started feeling dizzy because I didn't drink enough water and it was 98 degrees out.

density—*n*. the mass of an object divided by its volume. Just remember, light things are usually less <u>dense</u> than heavy things.

deteriorate—*v*. to get worse. When you hear someone say "his health is <u>deteriorating</u>," that means it is getting worse. When you hear someone say "that house is <u>deteriorating</u>," that means it is falling apart because no one is keeping it up.

digestive system—*n*. the parts of your body that work together to break down food so it can be converted into energy. Your <u>digestive system</u> is made up of the alimentary canal, which is basically every part of your body the food touches, from your mouth all the way down to . . . well, you know.

dilate—*v*. to get wide. Your pupils <u>dilate</u> when there isn't much light. That's because when they get wider, they can let more light in.

dissolve—*v*. to break into smaller parts and mix with a liquid. Kool Aid <u>dissolves</u> in water to make a tasty, refreshing drink!

distill—*v*. to purify by evaporation and then condensation. <u>Distilled</u> water has had all of the impurities boiled out. What they do is boil the water and then capture the steam—that steam doesn't have any of the impurities that were in the water. They then drop the temperature on the steam and—ta da!—<u>distilled</u> water.

dominant trait—*n*. when paired with a recessive trait, this is the trait that "wins"—the <u>dominant trait</u> beats the recessive trait. So if the <u>dominant trait</u> in a species of butterfly is big wings and the recessive trait is little wings, a butterfly that has one gene for each will have big wings.

dormant—*adj*. sleeping; inactive. Lots of animals, insects, and plants go <u>dormant</u> over the winter, sleeping until spring. When the Marlins' bats go <u>dormant</u>, that means no one is getting any hits, and the team is doomed.

ecosystem—*n*. the combination of organisms and the place they live. My backyard is an <u>ecosystem</u> all by itself. It has my dad's Koi

WhizTip

Whenever you see a word with "plasm" in it, you know it has something to do with cells.

WhizTip

I have found that when I don't read regularly, my vocabulary starts to deteriorate.

Science

Name three organisms that are part of an ecosystem at or near your house.
1.
2.
3.

pond filled with goldfish and frogs, my mom's lemon trees, and all the bugs and other animals that call my backyard home. There are probably hundreds of species of plants and animals making up the ecosystem back there.

efficient—*adj.* not wasting time or energy. I have often found that I study most efficiently when there is no noise. If I turn on the radio or TV, it takes me forever to get anything done.

electron—*n.* a tiny particle in an atom's nucleus that has a negative charge. There are the same number of protons (+) and electrons (−) in an atom's nucleus. Their opposite charges cancel each other out.

endocrine system—*n.* the body's endocrine glands, ductless organs that secrete hormones directly into the blood. The endocrine system includes the thyroid, pituitary, and adrenal glands, plus a bunch more I don't have room to list here. (See "The Body" in the science exercises for all of the components.)

endothermic—*adj.* absorbing heat. Think of indoors for endothermic reactions. It's a reaction that brings heat "inside."

exothermic—adj. releasing heat. Think of an EXIT sign for exothermic reactions.

entropy—*n.* disorder or chaos in a system. So if the Orlando Magic have three injured players, they have entropy on the team—disorder and chaos.

epicenter—*n.* the location directly over the center of an earthquake. You hear the word on the nightly news all the time when they are talking about earthquakes, like "The epicenter of the earthquake is located 150 miles west of San Diego, right here where I am standing! Aaaaaaahhhggggghhh!" And then the camera fritzes off.

equilibrium—*n.* a condition in which all forces cancel each other out, resulting in balance. Remember it by thinking of the word "equal." Equilibrium happens when opposing forces are equal.

erosion—*n.* the process of soil being worn away, usually by water and wind.

eruption—*n.* the explosion of a volcano. The eruption of Mount Vesuvius in A.D. 79 ended up burying two entire cities in lava and ash. They have only recently started excavating the site.

Do an Internet search and find the most recent volcano eruption in the United States.

evaporation—*n.* the process of a liquid turning into a gas. I left a glass of Kool Aid on my bedroom window sill and forgot about it. A few weeks later, all the liquid had evaporated, and all that was left was red, crusty goo. (Also see the definitions for *distill* and *condensation point*.)

exothermic—*adj.* releasing heat. An exothermic reaction happens when substances react strongly with each other. For example, if you mix two substances in a test tube and the tube gets hot, that's an exothermic reaction. Heat has been released. (See *endothermic* for more on this.)

Name three more extinct animals or species.
1.
2.
3.

extinct—*adj.* no longer in existence. The dodo bird is extinct—there aren't any of them on the planet any more. Dinosaurs are extinct. My mom says real gentlemen are extinct. (I'm not sure what that means.)

extrapolate—*v.* to take things you know and make assumptions based on those things. If you have gotten As on all your science tests so far, you can <u>extrapolate</u> that you will get good grades on the rest of your science tests, too.

extraterrestrial—*adj.* outside the Earth. Lots of people think there are <u>extraterrestrial</u> beings in outer space. I think they're nuts.

fault—*n.* a break in a rock formation. Earthquakes happen along geologic <u>faults,</u> where a rock formation is broken and two big slabs of rock are rubbing against each other.

food chain—*n.* a line of organisms that eat each other.

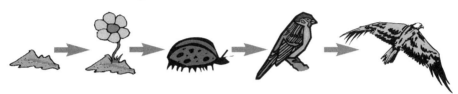

The <u>food chain</u> ends when an animal has no known predator—that means no other animals eat it. (Most hawks have nothing to fear.)

formation—*n.* an arrangement. In geology, a rock <u>formation</u> is an arrangement of rocks with particular characteristics.

fossil fuel—*n.* fuel made from decayed organisms. Coal and oil are actually dead plants and animals that decayed and have been compressed over millions of years into <u>fossil fuels</u>. Wind is not a <u>fossil fuel</u>. Neither is solar energy. They are renewable resources. (See the definition for *renewable*.)

friction—*n.* rough rubbing. The <u>friction</u> between two rock formations is what causes earthquakes.

fusion—*n.* in physics, a reaction where atoms join together. In chemistry, when two substances are melted and mixed together. Basically, <u>fusion</u> takes place when two separate things <u>combine</u> into one thing.

gene—*n.* a section of a chromosome that controls how part of an organism turns out. You have <u>genes</u> that control your eye color, your height, your looks—everything. And we are learning more and more about <u>genes</u> every day. Scientists just completed charting every <u>gene</u>—it was called the Human Genome Project.

generation—*n.* a group of people born around the same time; a stage in a succession. I have heard people calling our <u>generation</u> "Generation I" because we are the first to grow up with computers and the Internet.

generator—*n.* a machine that generates electricity. My dad has a <u>generator</u> in the garage for when we get blasted by hurricanes. Even when the hurricanes miss us, the power usually goes out for a little while and we have to power up the <u>generator</u>.

genetics—*n.* the study of genes and heredity. The field of <u>genetics</u> is really booming right now. All of the stuff they are finding out about genes and how they affect our health and everything about us

Whiz Quiz

Think of a name for your generation that is better than Generation I.

Science

is really cool. Some people even think <u>genetics</u> will be the key to curing cancer!

geology—*n.* the study of rocks and the Earth. If I don't make it as a major league pitcher, I think I'm going to be a <u>geologist</u>. I am almost as interested in earthquakes and volcanoes as I am in sports.

greenhouse effect—*n.* the result of too many pollutants in the atmosphere; they let the sunlight in, but they don't let the heat back out. That causes the atmosphere to act like a greenhouse—keeping the heat in. Some people think the <u>greenhouse effect</u> is causing all the glaciers around the polar icecaps to melt.

hemisphere—*n.* in earth sciences, the northern or southern half of the Earth. The equator is what separates the northern and southern <u>hemispheres</u>. To remember it, think <u>hemisphere</u> = half-a-sphere.

herbivore—*n.* an animal that eats plants. Cows are <u>herbivores</u>. Horses are <u>herbivores</u>. Vegetarians are <u>herbivores</u>. They all eat veggies, no meats.

hybrid—*n.* the offspring you get when you breed two different kinds of parents. You most often hear the word <u>hybrid</u> when people are talking about plants, like a corn <u>hybrid</u> that fends off insects or a <u>hybrid</u> tomato that is bigger and juicier than any other kind of tomato ever.

hydroelectric—*adj.* relating to electricity generated by water turning a turbine. My aunt in New York works at a public radio station that is run on <u>hydroelectric</u> power! All their power comes from a dam in a river outside the station.

hydrosphere—*n.* the world's waters. All the oceans, seas, lakes, rivers, streams, and puddles make up the <u>hydrosphere</u>.

hypothesis—*n.* a proposed explanation or statement. Scientific progress is based on proving or disproving a <u>hypothesis</u>. If your <u>hypothesis</u> is "plants are mean," and you do an experiment that proves plants are mean, then your hypothesis is correct. If the experiment does not prove plants are mean, that DOES NOT mean the <u>hypothesis</u> is incorrect, only that your experiment didn't prove it.

igneous rock—*n.* rock that is formed from molten lava. It's not metamorphic, it's not sedimentary—it's igneous! (See the definition for <u>rock cycle</u>.)

ignite—*v.* to light on fire. When you <u>ignite</u> your Bunsen burner in science class, it gives off a blue flame.

immune—*adj.* being resistant to something bad. You often hear this word when people are talking about AIDS. AIDS is an acronym for Acquired Immunodeficiency Syndrome. It's a disease that attacks your <u>immune</u> system, and makes it so you can't fight off any bacteria or other bad germs.

incinerate—*v.* to burn until there is nothing left but ashes. If you flew a space shuttle toward the sun, the sun's heat would <u>incinerate</u> it.

inertia—*n.* resistance to motion. My dad has a lot of <u>inertia</u> on weekends. It's hard to get him off the couch.

Whiz Fact

The United Nations did an environmental study that concluded that the greenhouse effect is going to raise the average temperature of the Earth two to ten degrees in the next 100 years.

DOUBLE MEANING

hemisphere—n. also stands for one-half of the brain—the left and right hemispheres.

Whiz Fact

There is a big debate about what to do with the dams in the West that produce hydroelectric power. Some want to destroy them and restore the rivers—and the fish.

Whiz Quiz

Identify the rock's type:

basalt
_____

granite
_____

limestone
_____

marble
_____

inexhaustible—*adj.* never ending. It may seem like the earth has an <u>inexhaustible</u> supply of oil and coal, but that's not true. If we keep going the way we are going now, we will be out of oil and coal in just a few hundred years. Then what?

infrared—*adj.* radiation that has waves shorter than microwaves and greater than visible light. Most television remotes use <u>infrared</u> technology to make your television do your bidding.

insulation—*n.* protective material. There are lots of different kinds of <u>insulation</u> in your house. Heat <u>insulation</u> keeps heat from escaping your house. Water pipe <u>insulation</u> keeps them from freezing when it's cold. There is also <u>insulation</u> around electrical wires that keeps the wires from shocking everything they touch!

What's another kind of insulation? Try to think of one.

interact—*v.* to be involved with something else. Science is always testing how different things <u>interact</u>. It can be chemicals that <u>interact</u> with each other in an experiment, it can be animals <u>interacting</u> with each other in a habitat, it can be how the orbits of planets <u>interact</u> with each other.

ion—*n.* an atom or molecule that used to be electrically neutral, but now it is either positive or negative because it gained or lost electrons. In other words, it used to be neutral (same number of protons and electrons) but it has since gained or lost an electron, so it is a positive <u>ion</u> (lost electrons) or negative <u>ion</u> (gained electrons).

kinetic—*adj.* having to do with movement. Most often, it is used to describe <u>kinetic</u> energy. Example: When my 3-wood smacks my Titleist 180 yards, that's <u>kinetic</u> energy. Another way to remember <u>kinetic</u> is to think of *calisthenics*. They kind of sound the same, and they both have to do with movement.

land subsidence—*n.* the sinking of land. In some arid regions of the Southwest, tapping the water in the water table has resulted in <u>land subsidence</u>. As water is sucked out, the land actually sinks!

laser—*n.* a device that emits a ray of invisible radiation. <u>Laser</u> is an acronym for (L)ight (A)mplification by (S)timulated (E)mission of (R)adiation.

lethal—*adj.* causing death. Some states with capital punishment, like Texas, use a <u>lethal</u> injection to kill the prisoners on death row.

List three things that are lethal to humans:
1. _____
2. _____
3. _____

light year—*n.* the distance light travels in a vacuum in one year (9.46×10^{12} kilometers). It's important to remember that a <u>light year</u> is a measure of distance, not time.

lithosphere—*n.* the Earth's crust. All of the valleys, mountains, plains, and meadows, plus all of the bottoms of the seas, rivers, and lakes, make up the <u>lithosphere</u>.

lunar—*adj.* having to do with the moon. A <u>lunar</u> eclipse is when the Earth blocks the sun's light to the moon. The <u>lunar</u> module is a spaceship that landed on the moon.

magma—*n.* the molten rock below the Earth's surface, waiting to spew out in a volcano and then form igneous rock when it cools. I went on a vacation to Hawaii and I actually saw red, glowing <u>magma</u> where there are active volcanoes.

magnitude—*n.* a measure of the amount of energy released by an earthquake. Earthquakes' <u>magnitudes</u> are always measured. Small earthquakes have <u>magnitudes</u> from 2–3. Medium-size earthquakes have <u>magnitudes</u> from 4–6. Large earthquakes have magnitudes from 7–10.

mantle—*n.* the layer of rock between the Earth's crust and its core. So, we walk all over the crust, the core is boiling molten rock, and the only thing keeping the molten rock from us crust-dwellers is the <u>mantle</u>. Thank you, <u>mantle</u>!

meiosis—*n.* cell division in sexually reproducing organisms that produces a cell with half the required number of chromosomes that will then link up with the other half of the chromosomes from the other sex partner. Humans have 46 chromosomes—23 from each parent. <u>Meiosis</u> is what produces one of those 23-chromosome sex cells (called gametes).

membrane—*n.* as in cell membrane, the outer layer of the cell. The <u>membrane</u> keeps all the stuff inside the cell from floating out AND it keeps out the stuff the cell doesn't need.

metabolism—*n.* the chemical and physical processes that take place in cells; the changes that take place in the body. You have probably heard people say "I have a high <u>metabolism</u>—I eat anything I want all day and I don't gain a pound." Someone with a high <u>metabolism</u> has a body that is working really fast and efficiently to burn up all the food it gets.

Related Word

metamorphosis—n. the change from one thing to another.

metamorphic rock—*n.* rock that was changed from one kind of rock to another by pressure or temperature. It's not sedimentary, it's not igneous—it's <u>metamorphic</u>! (See the definition for <u>rock cycle</u>.)

Related Word

meteorite—n. a space rock that enters the Earth's atmosphere and makes a meteor.

meteor—*n.* the trail behind a meteorite caused by the meteorite entering the Earth's atmosphere. Last year I saw the most awesome <u>meteor</u> shower I have ever seen. There were so many <u>meteors</u> burning up as they entered our atmosphere, it was like the sky was on fire.

microwave—*n.* an electromagnetic wave that has a wavelength between infrared and a short-wave radio. Of course, you have probably used a <u>microwave</u> oven a few times here and there, so you know what these <u>microwaves</u> can do. Cook!

WhizFact

Mineral water is plain old water infused with some minerals that are good for you.

mineral—*n.* a natural substance with a definite chemical and crystalline composition. A diamond is a <u>mineral</u>. So are gold and silver.

mitochondrion—*n.* the part of the cell that converts food into energy the body can use. It's at the last stage of digestion, working to turn that burger and fries into energy for your body.

mitosis—*n.* the division of a cell into two separate cells; the differentiation and segregation of replicated chromosomes in a cell's nucleus.

molecule—*n.* the smallest unit of a compound or an element. A water <u>molecule</u> has two hydrogens and one oxygen atom—H_2O.

molten—*adj.* melted or liquefied by intense heat. The lava that comes out of volcanoes is <u>molten</u> rock.

Related Word

magma **(See its definition.)**

mutation—*n.* a change in the genes of an organism from one generation to the next. The theory of evolution states that a <u>mutation</u> that helps an organism survive better than others will be passed down from generation to generation, because that organism and its offspring will have a better chance of living and having kids. That's why giraffes have long necks. They lived in a place where the food was up high, so the ones with the genetic <u>mutation</u> that gave them longer necks did better and had more kids, while the ones with shorter necks couldn't get to the food, and eventually died off.

Whiz Quiz

Name a genetic mutation **that helped this species survive:**

giraffe
human
elephant
cheetah

natural selection—*n.* the theory that organisms best suited for their environment survive and have offspring, and those who are not die and do not have offspring. Also known as "survival of the fittest." Kind of harsh, I know. But it is the way things work in nature. (See *mutation* for more on this.)

neutron—*n.* a particle that's in the nucleus of all atoms (except hydrogen.) A <u>neutron</u> has the same mass as a proton, but no electrical charge (it is neutral). So the nuclei of atoms have protons, electrons, and <u>neutrons</u> (except hydrogen).

nuclear energy—*n.* the energy released by a nuclear reaction. <u>Nuclear energy</u> makes up a big part of this country's energy production, but not nearly as much as energy produced by burning oil, coal, and natural gas. The thing is, <u>nuclear energy</u> plants can be more dangerous than other energy sources. If something goes wrong and radiation escapes from nuclear power plant, people can get sick and die.

Whiz Fact

Famous dangerous nuclear **accidents:**

Three-Mile Island, 1979 Pennsylvania, USA

Chernobyl, 1986 Chernobyl, Ukraine

nucleus—*n.* 1) in a cell, the center of a cell containing the genes. The <u>nucleus</u> of a cell contains the parts that control the cell, like the <u>nucleus</u> of a baseball team is made up of the players who control whether a team wins or loses. 2) In an atom, the center of the atom containing protons, electrons, and neutrons.

nutrients—*n.* the stuff that nourishes your body. You see the word all the time on vitamin commercials—"VitaMight contains 127 essential <u>nutrients</u> to keep your body glowing like a lightbulb!" The fact is you get plenty of <u>nutrients</u> from the foods you eat, as long as you eat the right foods.

orbit—*n.* the path of one celestial body around another. Planets travel in their different <u>orbits</u> around the sun.

organic—*adj.* having to do with living organisms. When you see food labeled "organic" in the grocery store, that means it was grown with all <u>organic</u> materials—no chemicals or man-made substances were used.

organism—*n.* a living plant, animal, bacterium, protist, or fungus. I have used the word <u>organism</u> in tons of these science definitions. It's obviously because lots of science is concerned with the study of <u>organisms</u> and all of the things that affect <u>organisms</u>.

oxidation—*n.* a reaction in which the atoms in an element lose electrons. The most common example of <u>oxidation</u> is the formation of rust. Metal atoms <u>oxidize</u>—they lose electrons—and rust forms.

ozone layer—*n.* a layer of our atmosphere that protects us from harmful sun rays. Pollution is causing holes in the <u>ozone layer</u>, which means those bad sun rays are making it all the way down to the Earth, where they can cause skin cancer. My mom always makes me wear sunscreen when I play baseball because she's worried about the holes in the <u>ozone layer</u>.

patent—*n.* a pledge made by a government that says an inventor has the sole right to make, sell, and use his invention for a period of time. So Thomas Edison had a <u>patent</u> on his light bulbs for a period of time, then a few years later his invention became available to everyone, and anyone who wanted could make a light bulb.

periodic table—*n.* the chart that lists all of the elements and their atomic numbers.

5	6	7	8
B	C	N	O
13	14	15	16
Al	Si	P	S
31	32	33	34
Ga	Ge	As	Se

pH—*n.* a measure of how acidic or alkaline a substance is.

photosynthesis—*n.* the process plants use to turn sunlight into energy. If people could perform <u>photosynthesis</u>, we wouldn't need to eat so much! We could just sit in the sun and get all the energy we need. Instead we have to cover ourselves in sunscreen and stay in the shade. Lucky plants!

porous—*adj.* penetrable by liquid or gas. A sponge is <u>porous</u>. A bowling ball is not <u>porous</u>.

precipitation—*n.* rain, snow, sleet, and hail. The weatherman said the odds of <u>precipitation</u> tomorrow are 50 percent. But he's never right.

Related Word

predatory—adj.
like a hunter.

predator—*n.* an animal that hunts another. A shark is a fierce <u>predator</u>, hunting other fish continuously, never sleeping, always hungry.

proton—*n.* a positively charged particle in an atom. (See definitions of *electron* and *neutron*.)

protoplasm—*n.* a jellylike substance that forms all the living matter in plants and animals. That's right, the basis for all living things is a jiggly mass of jelly. Kind of gross when you think about it, so I try not to.

protozoa—*n.* primitive, single-celled organisms. <u>Protozoa</u> might be what the earliest forms of life on Earth were like.

radiation—*n.* the emission of waves or particles. Nuclear <u>radiation</u> is waves and particles given off by radioactive material. It can be really dangerous and even lethal.

recessive trait—*n.* when paired with a dominant trait, it is the trait that "loses." (See the definition of *dominant trait* for more.)

renewable—*adj.* able to be used again. Most often used in the term "<u>renewable</u> resources" to describe sources of energy that can be used again and again. Two examples are wind and sunlight—they are forms of energy that you can use over and over, and they never get used up.

replicate—*v.* to copy. After fertilization in sexual reproduction, cells start <u>replicating</u> themselves, and an embryo is formed.

reproduction—*n.* the process by which living things produce offspring. Most animals and plants use sexual <u>reproduction</u>, where the offspring gets half its chromosomes from each parent. In asexual <u>reproduction</u>, the offspring gets all its genetic material from one parent. The formation of spores by certain bacteria, fungi, and algae is a good example of asexual <u>reproduction</u>.

resistant—*adj.* able to fight off something. Some crops are engineered to be <u>resistant</u> to certain bugs. Some <u>bacteria</u> become resistant to drugs that are used to kill them. So <u>resistance</u> can be good for us (crops that can fend off pests) and bad for us (diseases that are <u>resistant</u> to treatment).

respiratory system—*n.* the group of organs that keep you breathing. If you think of it in terms of your house, things that circulate air—like fans and air-conditioners—are your house's respiratory system. (See the "The Body" exercise for all of the organs involved in your <u>respiratory system</u>.).

rock cycle—*n.* a rock's "life" cycle, in which a rock goes from igneous to sedimentary to metamorphic by going through erosion, crushing, pressure, melting, and everything else rocks goes through.

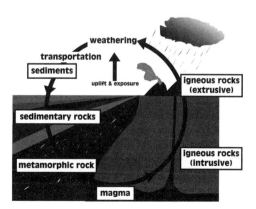

weathering
transportation
sediments
uplift & exposure
igneous rocks (extrusive)
sedimentary rocks
igneous rocks (intrusive)
metamorphic rock
magma

Science

satellite—*n.* a man-made object shot into space that orbits the Earth or another planet. Most satellites these days are used for communication, but there are also science satellites and military satellites.

scientific method—*n.* the process of observing something, forming a hypothesis for how it works, doing experiments to test that hypothesis, and then drawing conclusions from your results. *Example*: If from watching bears at the zoo you form the hypothesis that bears are dumb as rocks, and you do an experiment to test them. Maybe you ask them their names. When the bears don't answer, you conclude your hypothesis is correct—they don't know their names, so they must be dumb as rocks. (You can see why the scientific method isn't perfect!)

sedimentary rock—*n.* rock that is formed near the Earth's surface by the accumulation of sediment. It's not *metamorphic*, it's not *igneous*—it's sedimentary! (See the definition for *rock cycle*.)

selective breeding—*n.* the process of choosing which plants or animals to breed with each other. You do this when you are looking to promote a particular trait. So if you are breeding poodles and you want poodles with extra long toes, you selectively breed the long-toed poodles. (You give the short-toed poodles away to friends.)

solar—*adj.* having to do with the sun. The solar system is the system of planets revolving around the sun. Solar flares are eruptions that spew from the sun and mess up our television reception. Solarcaine stops sunburn pain when someone you love is hurting.

soluble—*adj.* dissolvable. Sugar is soluble in water. So is Kool Aid.

stagnant—*adj.* motionless; not flowing. When water is stagnant, it becomes a prime breeding ground for mosquitoes. When the Florida Marlins' offense is stagnant, that means we need to get some better hitters on the team.

stimulus—*n.* something that causes a response. An organism is always responding to both internal and external stimuli. For example, a toad responds to external stimuli like predators and temperature and internal stimuli like hunger and the urge to reproduce.

sustainable—*adj.* able to maintain over a period of time. One of the ways to fight world hunger is to find sustainable crops that starving countries can grow themselves. There is a Chinese proverb that explains this: "Give a man a fish and he will eat for a day. Teach a man to fish and he will eat for the rest of his life."

synthesis—*n.* the combination of two or more things to make a brand new thing. I think the *Star Wars* movies are the perfect synthesis of special effects and a great story. Combining those two things has made a brand new thing—the best movie series ever.

tectonic plates—*n.* the huge plates that make up the continents and the floors of the oceans. They shift a little all of the time. The friction where the tectonic plates meet causes scary stuff to happen, including earthquakes, mountains, and tidal waves.

temperate—*adj.* not hot, not cold. This word is most often used when talking about <u>temperate</u> climates, where animals and plants thrive because the temperature does not get too hot or cold.

texture—*n.* the feeling and appearance of a surface. My new cotton sweater has a smooth <u>texture</u>. My old wool sweater had a rough <u>texture</u>. Plus it was hotter than Key West in August.

topography—*adj.* the physical aspects of a place or region. The word is often used in the phrase "<u>topographical</u> map," which is a map that shows a region's physical landscape instead of roads and landmarks.

toxic—*adj.* harmful; dangerous. Scientists deal with toxic materials all of the time. Sometimes we even work with them in science class ourselves. Stuff like mercury and dry ice are pretty cool, but they can be very <u>toxic</u>, so be careful.

transform—*v.* to change from one thing into another. Coal is <u>transformed</u> into diamonds under intense pressure after millions of years.

vacuum—*n.* a space where there is no matter. Lots of science experiments have to be done in a <u>vacuum</u> to work. For example, in a <u>vacuum</u>, a feather and a brick fall at the same rate, because there is no matter—air—to make the feather float more slowly.

vapor—*n.* stuff that looks like mist, fumes, or smoke. Steam is the <u>vapor</u> form of water.

virus—*n.* a tiny parasite that lives and replicates inside another organism. <u>Viruses</u> can be deadly (the HIV virus that causes AIDS) or relatively harmless (common cold) depending on how easily the immune system can kill them.

watt—*n.* the fleshy orange fold of skin under a turkey's neck. Wait—that's a wattle! A <u>watt</u> is a unit of electricity. If you want to save electricity, change all the light bulbs in your house to 40-<u>watt</u> or 60-<u>watt</u> bulbs.

Think of Goldilocks: not too hot and not too cold, the "temperate porridge" is just right!

Nature is full of transformations. Name three:

1. _____
2. _____
3. _____

WhizWords

acclimatization
conservation
ecosystem
fossil fuel
greenhouse effect
organism

Science
The Environment

Related Word

renewable—adj.
Fossil fuels are
not renewable.
You use them
once, and they
are history.

Have you ever heard of Woody Guthrie? He was a folk singer who wrote hundreds of songs about America. He would travel the country hitchhiking and riding on freight trains, getting to know the people he met along the way. He ended up writing classics like "This Land Is Your Land," "Pastures of Plenty," and "Do-Re-Mi." (No, not the song about "a female deer" and "a drop of golden sun." A different "Do-Re-Mi.")

Guthrie was also a big environmentalist. He was really alarmed by all of the factories he saw going up around the country. He saw America as an expanse of forests and plains and deserts and lakes and rivers. And he saw it changing into an expanse of roads and cities and houses and, well, people.

My dad loves Woody Guthrie. He is always humming "This Land Is Your Land" and putting in his own words. So when he has to cut the grass, he likes to sing "This land is your land, this land is my land, I've got to cut the grass, that'll keep me smilin'." It can get annoying, but it gave me a great idea for how to remember environment words.

WRITE A FOLK SONG EXERCISE

What I want you to do is use each of these environment words in a verse of "This Land Is Your Land." You want to squish the word and the definition into the verse. It may not win you any Grammys, but if you spend some time on it and fit all six words into six verses, you'll have a little hummable song about the environment. And you can hum it during a test if you need to remember the words!

I'll get you started with a verse about the WhizWord off to the side— <u>fossil fuel</u>.

♪ This land is your land,
this land is my land, ♫
<u>Fossil fuel</u> emits carbon monoxide,
when you burn it in your car, man.

If you have another song you want to use instead of "This Land Is Your Land," by all means, go ahead. If you've never even heard "This Land Is Your Land," ask your music teacher to hum a few bars, or go on the Internet to *www.geocities.com/Nashville/3448/thisl1.html* to hear a snippet.

Science

The Body

By the end of middle school you should have a pretty good idea of what the different parts of the body do. The four main systems of the body aren't that hard to understand, but there are a lot of organs in each one, so it's good to be able to organize the organs by the systems they are in.

Just remember: the **circulatory system** has to do with **circulating** the blood. The **digestive system** has to do with organs that help you **digest** your food. The **respiratory system** does your breathing for you (to remember the word, think about being put on a **respirator**—a machine that breathes for you). And the **endocrine system**, well, it helps get the bad stuff out of your blood. Crime is bad—so think about the endocrine system getting the bad stuff out of your blood. Close enough!

DRAWING YOUR INNARDS EXERCISE

I have listed the major organs in each system. Your challenge is to label them in this Britney Spears body outline. Check the answer key when you are done.

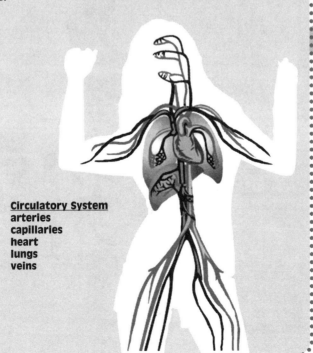

Circulatory System
arteries
capillaries
heart
lungs
veins

Science

Digestive System →
anus
esophagus
large intestine
mouth
small intestine
stomach

Respiratory System →
diaphragm
lungs
nose
pharynx (throat)
ribcage
trachea

The Body

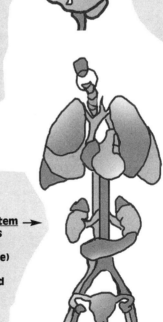

Endocrine System →
adrenal glands
hypothalamus
ovaries (female)
pancreas
pituitary gland
testes (male)
thyroid gland

WhizWords

asteroids
extraterrestrial
light year
lunar
meteor
orbit
satellite

Science

The Universe

Sometimes I just lie on my back in my backyard at night and look up at the sky and imagine what the astronauts on the International Space Station must think when they look out the window. Have you ever seen the movie *Apollo 13* or spent any time on NASA's website? The pictures of space from the windows of spacecraft are just incredible.

And now it looks like normal citizens are going to be able to go into space, just like the astronauts. In 2001 an American businessman named Dennis Tito became the first space tourist when he paid $20 million to join a Russian space crew on a trip to the International Space Station. So someday, you may get to travel in space, whether you're an astronaut or not.

DRAWING THE UNIVERSE EXERCISE

For this exercise you get to draw and label the universe, from the perspective of an astronaut on the old Mir. I have provided the Earth, its moon and the sun. You can draw and/or label the rest of the "Universe" words above. For example:

LABEL OR DRAW
distance to sun in light years
a meteor
the lunar orbit
asteroids
a satellite

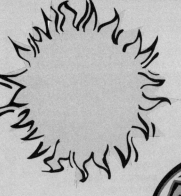

WhizWords
**dominant trait
gene
genetics
recessive trait**

Science

Genetics

My friend Gene has curly red hair and freckles just like his father and all of his brothers. That's how I remember that a **gene** is the part of the cell that decides which characteristics will be passed from one generation to the next.

But sometimes **genetics** don't work out quite so logically. For instance, my sister Jenny is really tall: 5'9". Both of my parents are short. So am I. So what happened to Jenny? There must have been a **recessive** "tall" **gene** that both of my parents carried that, against the odds, made it into my sister. The same goes for her eye color. My parents both have brown eyes. I have brown eyes. My sister has blue eyes. So what happened to Jenny? Again, a **recessive trait** in both my parents ended up being expressed in my freaky sister. Here's how that happens:

Whiz Tip
**See *Innerspace!*
It's a movie that came out in 1987 about a Navy pilot who gets minia-turized and injected into the body of a hypochondriac.**

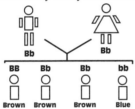

As you can see, the odds are great that my parents would have children with brown eyes, because that is the **dominant** gene for eye color. All you need is one brown eyes gene to have brown eyes. Jenny just got lucky and was the one kid who got a **recessive** "blue eyes" gene from each of my parents.

MOVIE AND TV STAR RECESSIVE TRAITS EXERCISE

Pick out two movie stars. I am going to pick Cher and Billy Crystal. Now, pick a trait. I am going to pick foot size and make big feet dominant and little feet recessive. Draw a chart like the one I drew above, giving each either two dominant genes (FF), two recessives (ff), or one of each (Ff). See how their children would turn out. Here is my Billy + Cher drawing.

I don't even want to think about what the rest of their bodies would look like.

WhizWords

continental drift
erosion
fault
geology
mantle
tectonic plates

Science

Geology

WhizTip

Want to learn about Florida's geology? Start by checking out the Florida Geological Survey at www.dep.state.fl.us.geo.

Living in Florida, you can forget that the world is a big mass of sliding plates drifting toward and away from each other, causing havoc where they butt up against each other. Everything here is pretty idyllic, except for the stray hurricane. But anyone who has studied the history of the Earth—and anyone who lives in California—knows that beneath us is a molten core of boiling rock, yearning to break free!

When you think of it this way, **geology** is pretty cool. In addition to studying the process of **continental drift**, geologists get to hunt for wild-looking fossils and try to piece them together like giant jigsaw puzzles. You can see why there are so many geologists running around, predicting earthquakes and digging up dinosaurs.

EARTHQUAKE EXERCISE

Unfortunately, geology is not always fun and games. Every once in a while a big earthquake hits and people lose their homes and sometimes their lives. The same forces that create mountains also create terrible tragedies.

For this exercise, I want you to research a recent earthquake. There was a massive earthquake in India in 2001 that killed tens of thousands. There was also an earthquake in San Francisco in 1989 that ruined the freeway system and caused a World Series game that was taking place when it hit to be postponed.

Once you have compiled some information on an earthquake, turn the page. Write a short essay in the space provided using the words above to explain the tectonic shifts that caused the trembler. Underline the WhizWords in the essay.

Essay

EXPLAIN THE TECTONIC SHIFTS BEHIND A RECENT EARTHQUAKE.

Chapter 5

Test Instructions

Use your pencil when you have reading passages on tests. Underline the topic sentence of each paragraph and circle proper names. It will help slow you down and help you when you refer back to the passage for information.

Circle your answer to the following best questions: Which word best describes President Bush?

man woman child

What is your best prediction of how the Marlins will do this year?

better worse same

Which word best supports this sentence: "Miami is the capital of Florida."

right maybe wrong

according to the passage—When you see this phrase, you know the answer to the question is right in the passage you just read. You don't have to use your imagination or remember what you learned in class to find an answer. The answer to the question is in the reading passage.

accurate—*adj.* exactly right. As in "Which of the following is an accurate statement?" This means "Which statement matches the information given?" *Example*: If the information says Jenny spit out her broccoli when her mom wasn't looking because broccoli makes her sick, an accurate statement would be "Jenny can't stand broccoli," NOT "Jenny can't stand her mother."

approximate—*v.* to come close to; to estimate. Sometimes tests ask you to approximate—that means you are supposed to use the information they give you to make an estimate. Estimates are answers that are close to the real answer. When your car breaks down, the repair shop gives an estimate on how much the repairs will cost. This is approximately how much it will cost. It may be a little more, it may be a little less.

author's purpose—the writer's reason for writing, as in "the author's purpose in this passage is to . . . ." In "author's purpose" questions, you are looking for what the author was trying to accomplish with his writing. Sometimes an author's purpose is to scare you (horror novel). Sometimes an author's purpose is to convince you to believe something (persuasive article). Think about how you felt after reading the passage—how you felt is probably the author's purpose.

best—*adj.* you'll see this word a lot: "best represents;" "best estimate;" "best evidence;" "best characterizes;" "the best summary;" "best supported by information in the passage." It means you have to use your "best judgment" and pick the "best answer." You may have a set of answer choices that all seem like they could be right, and you have to choose the one that is the best (more right than the others).

compare and contrast—show the similarities and the differences. Tests love for you to compare and contrast things because it's a great way for them to figure out if you understand what you are reading and writing.

complete the pattern—also seen on tests as "if the pattern continues . . . ." This phrase is used on number pattern questions. The test is asking you to find the next number in a number pattern. Figure out what the pattern is, and fill in the next—or missing— number to <u>complete the pattern</u>.

contribute to the development—to further. As in "How do the doctor's comments to Frank <u>contribute to the development</u> of the story?"

convince—*v.* to persuade. As in "information to <u>convince</u> the reader..." Some tests ask you if an author provided enough examples to convince you of something. So if I wanted to <u>convince</u> you the Marlins are going to win the World Series this year, I'd have to provide a ton of reasons to persuade you.

corresponds—*v.* matches; agrees with. Sometimes you are asked to pick the answer that <u>corresponds</u> to the data in the question. That just means it matches. So a test may have a statement like:

The *Star Wars* Trilogy became the highest grossing movie series ever, earning more than $1 billion.

And then it says:

Pick the statement that <u>corresponds</u> to the data given in the statement:

    A) The *Star Wars* trilogy lost money.

    B) The *Star Wars* trilogy won three Oscars.

    C) The *Star Wars* trilogy made a lot of money.

equivalent—*adj.* the same as. Test questions—especially math and science test questions—often want you to find things that are <u>equivalent</u> to one another. That just means finding an answer that is the same as something in the question. So if a test wants you to find the <u>equivalent</u> to a dozen eggs, you pick 12 eggs. If a test wants you to find the <u>equivalent</u> of 1/2 meter, you pick 50 centimeters.

expression—*n.* a way of saying something, usually using an

> **Related Word**
> The word **corresponds** **is related to the words** accurate, equivalent, **and** exactly.

Whiz Quiz

Circle the facts, underline the opinions:

The Marlins won the World Series in 1997.

They are going to win it again this year.

The Marlins beat the Braves for the NL pennant on their way to the World Series in 1997.

The Marlins will beat the Braves every time they meet next year.

Charles Johnson is the best catcher in the Major Leagues.

Whiz Tip

Think of the main idea as the "main tent" at a circus. That's where the main show with the elephants and the trapeze artists is. The other parts of the circus are in smaller tents. They are all part of the circus, but the main tent is the main idea. So when you look at the answer choices, think "Is this the elephant in the main tent, or the bearded lady in a smaller tent?"

equation. As in "which <u>expression</u> could be used" or "which <u>expression</u> represents the amount of money spent." So you are trying to match the <u>expression</u> to the passage. A passage may say:

Tim bought five eggs, dropped three, and then purchased five more. Which <u>expression</u> represents Tim's egg-buying experience?

A) 5 + 3 + 5

B) 5 − 3 − 5

C) 5 − 3 + 5

fact—*n.* something that actually happened or actually exists. As in "Which of these is a <u>fact</u> in this passage?" *Note*: When there is a question about a <u>fact</u>, there is often also a question about *opinion*, too. (See the definition of *opinion*.)

greatest–least / greater than–less than—as in "What is the <u>greatest</u> number of (objects)" and "How much was the winning time in the race <u>greater than</u> the second place time?"

justify—*v.* to provide reasons for. As in "Use the information from all three circle graphs to <u>justify</u> your answer."

main idea—as in "The <u>main idea</u> of the story." You get a <u>main idea</u> by reading a passage carefully. Sometimes the title of a reading passage offers a clue about the <u>main idea</u>. Sometimes it's better to decide the passage's <u>main idea</u> *before* you read the answer choices. You will usually find your <u>main idea</u> among the answer choices. But if you read the answer choices first, it can get confusing, because usually all the ideas in the answer choices are in the passage, but they aren't the <u>main idea</u>.

measure—*n.* the size or shape. As in "What is the <u>measure</u>, in degrees, of angle CDE?"

nearest—*adj.* closest. As in "What is the new length, to the <u>nearest</u> inch, after the increase?"

opinion—*n.* something someone believes or thinks, whether it is true or not. As in "Which is an <u>opinion</u> in this passage?"

probably—*adv.* most likely. As in "How does the author <u>probably</u> feel about race car drivers?" It just means that the passage doesn't actually state what a character or writer believes, but from reading it, you should be able to tell anyway.

reason to believe—as in "gives the reader <u>reason to believe</u> . . . ." This means the passage makes you think one way, not the other way. For example, here's a sample passage: "The Miami Dolphins have drafted the 10 best players in college football, and the other teams in the NFL weren't allowed to draft anyone at all." This passage gives you <u>reason to believe</u> that:

A) The Dolphins will get better.

B) The other teams in the NFL will get better.

The answer is (A). You have <u>reason to believe</u> that if the Dolphins

got all the good players and the other teams didn't get any players at all, the Dolphins will get better, not the other teams, even though it doesn't actually say that in the passage.

represent—*v.* to stand for; to take the place of. As in "Let *x* <u>represent</u> the length of the pool."

rounded to the nearest—as in "<u>rounded to the nearest</u> thousand." When a test question asks you to round off, that means you go to the place given (tens, hundreds, thousands) and round up or down. If the next number is 5 or higher, you round up 1. If the next number is 4 or lower, you round down 1. On "<u>rounded to the nearest</u>" questions, it's very important to pay attention to whether the question is asking you to round to tens, hundreds, thousands, or whatever.

same meaning—as in "Which sentence below uses the word *burp* with the <u>same meaning</u> as the sentence from the passage?"

suggests—*v.* leads you to believe. As in "The information in the passage <u>suggests</u> . . . ." This just means the information doesn't come right out and say something, it just hints at it. It's kind of like a "probably" question—you have to read the passage carefully and trust your understanding of it.

support—*v.* to prove or provide evidence for. As in "<u>Support</u> your answer with details from the story."

weakest—*adj.* the least strong. As in "Which statement is the <u>weakest</u> argument for using toothpaste?"

Trust your instincts on these probably **questions. If you** probably **think a writer** probably **meant to say the Earth is flat, and that is an answer choice, you are** probably **right.**

WhizWords

according to the passage
author's purpose
best
main idea
support

Test Instructions
Reading Carefully

Related Word

conclude—v. to
reach an answer.
Tests are always
asking you
what you can
conclude from a
reading passage.

As you know by now, being able to read things and understand what you read is very important to doing well on the FCAT and other tests. The way tests figure out how well you are understanding things is by using these "Reading Carefully" phrases. So it helps if you get used to answering questions that use these words, not matter what kind of reading it is.

My favorite things to read are, in order, the online *Miami Herald* sports page, *Sports Illustrated,* and the *Harry Potter* series. So as long as J. K. Rowling keeps pumping out books, the Magic keep playing basketball, and Tiger Woods keeps going strong, I am going to be reading for the rest of my life. You probably have some favorite reading materials, too. That's what we are going to use in this next exercise.

READING WHAT YOU LIKE EXERCISE

Open your favorite book, magazine, newspaper or website. Pick a passage or article that's about one to three pages long. If you use a website, print out the article. Read it carefully, using your pencil to circle important names and underline important sentences. Take your time, really "get into" the writing. When you are done reading, write four sentences that start with these words:

The author's purpose in writing this article is . . .
The word that best describes the topic of this passage is . . .
The main idea of this passage is . . .
According to the passage, the author thinks . . .

Do this with at least five different kinds of writing. If you like doing it, do it a lot. It takes, like, five extra minutes, and you'll end up remembering a ton more stuff about things you actually like.

Test Instructions

Probably

Not everything in life is absolutely, positively 100 percent obviously true. Come to think of it, almost nothing is. That means you have to get used to recognizing degrees of possibility.

For example, the Orlando Magic are **probably** going to be really good for a long time because they have the best young player in basketball, Tracy McGrady, and perennial All-Star Grant Hill. And it's reasonable to **suggest** that Britney Spears is going to be popular for a long time because she's so . . . talented.

What's my point? My point is that even if you don't know something is absolutely, positively, 100 percent obviously true, you can still **probably** know a whole bunch of things. And on tests, one of the keys to doing well is being able to figure out what the **best** answer is.

If you are having trouble on tests figuring out what is probably true, a good way to get some perspective on things is to think "What would Mr. Reasonable do?" And everyone knows who the most reasonable people on the planet are. Newscasters!

> **Related Word**
>
> approximate—v. to come close to; to estimate. Math tests often ask you to approximate something, which means using the information they give you to get an answer in a general range.

MR. REASONABLE EXERCISE

If you don't watch the nightly news already, take half an hour out of your busy schedule and watch the Big Three: CBS (Dan Rather), NBC (Tom Brokaw), and ABC (Peter Jennings). Pick the newscaster who strikes you as the most reasonable of the bunch—the guy who would probably pick the right answer on a test. Mine is Tom Brokaw. He seems like he would make a good, reasonable guess.

Now write your newscaster's name on the top of a piece of paper, sit down with a parent or friend, and watch the news. Have your news buddy write down four questions about news stories from the nightly news, using the four "Probably" words. For example:

What word best describes the expression on President Bush's face when a cell phone rang during his press conference?

According to the news story, what is probably going to happen to gas prices in the next few months?

Before you answer, think "How would Tom Brokaw answer?" Do this every night for a week, and you'll probably get the hang of the "Probably" words and questions.

<u>Hint:</u> One way to be sure you've come up with the right answer to one of these questions on a test is to write a response that includes the word "because." This will require you to go back to the reading passage to find information to prove your point. If you can't find evidence to back up your answer, you're probably wrong.

Chapter 6
All-Purpose Words

adjacent—*adj.* next to. The WhizQuizzes and WhizTips in this book are <u>adjacent</u> to the definitions.

collaborate—*v.* to work together. You learn best when you <u>collaborate</u> in the classroom. My science teacher has us <u>collaborate</u> on projects, but I've been having trouble getting anyone to work with me since I accidentally lit my lab partner's Skittles on fire with a Bunsen burner.

consistent—*adj.* steady; always the same. The best way to do well on tests is to be <u>consistent</u> with your studying. Cramming for tests may work once in a while, but in the end you won't remember as much.

constructive—*adj.* helpful. The word is most commonly used in the phrase "<u>constructive</u> criticism," which means you are doing something wrong, but the person telling you is only trying to help by pointing out your errors and showing you how to improve.

contradiction—*n.* something that disagrees with something else. You have probably heard the phrase "a <u>contradiction</u> in terms." That's when two words in a row <u>contradict</u> each other, like: "an easy test." Tests aren't usually easy. Tests also often ask you to find <u>contradictions</u> in stories and passages. That is where two statements or pieces of information do not agree with each other.

convenient—*adj.* easy; handy. This book is incredibly <u>convenient</u> to keep around. It's small and it has all the words you need to know. Just put it in your bookbag and keep it there. Whenever you have a question about a word, this book will be <u>conveniently</u> in your bag and you can look it up.

conventional—*adj.* normal; accepted. One phrase that's used a lot is "<u>conventional</u> wisdom," as in: <u>Conventional</u> wisdom says that short people aren't that good at basketball.

logical—*adj.* reasonable; making sense. <u>Logical</u> is kind of the opposite of emotional. When you get emotional on tests, you can really mess up. Try to stay <u>logical</u> as much as you can, going from one question to the next without getting too worked up.

objective—*adj.* fair; impartial. To remember this word, just

List the three classmates you collaborate with most often:

_____

_____

_____

inconvenient—adj. causing a lot of trouble.

think about what kind of opinions an "object" like a chair would have. Answer: no opinions, objects don't have opinions.

precise—*adj.* exact; accurate. Tests kind of go back and forth from asking you to be <u>precise</u> with your answers to asking you to estimate (make a reasonable guess). So make sure you pay attention to <u>precisely</u> what the test question asks for.

predict—*v.* to guess in advance. Some test questions ask you to <u>predict</u> what will happen in an experiment or in a story. That means you are supposed to look at the facts and make a logical conclusion as to what will happen. (See definitions of *logical* in this section and *conclusion* in Language Arts.)

relevant—*adj.* related to the matter at hand. Sometimes on tests, you are asked to use only <u>relevant</u> information—that means information that matters (as opposed to stuff that does not matter). For example, if you are taking a test on making cheese, milk is <u>relevant</u>, because it's an ingredient in cheese, while information on fingernails is not <u>relevant</u> (it is <u>irrelevant</u>).

strategic—*adj.* planned. This word is used a lot when talking about war—especially about generals' "<u>strategic</u> maneuvers." Chess is a game that also requires a lot of "<u>strategic</u> maneuvers." Speaking of which, when you are taking tests, it can be important for you to have a <u>strategy</u> going in, like "I am going to stay cool no matter what" or "I am going to do the easy questions first and the hard ones second." Both of those are good <u>strategies</u>.

systematic—*adj.* acting according to an organized plan. <u>Systematic</u> is a lot like *strategic*—they both are used a lot when talking about a powerful person, like a general or dictator, who has a master plan and a strategy or a system to carry it out.

tangible—*adj.* touchable; real. This book is <u>tangible</u>—it is real and you can touch it. The word is used a lot in the phrase "<u>tangible</u> benefits," which means good things that actually happen. For example, my friend Kevin realized the <u>tangible</u> benefits from all his time in the kitchen when he won first prize in the cake baking contest.

Try to predict your grade on a test before you take it, then see how close you are to your prediction.

Antonym

irrelevant—adj. not pertaining to the matter at hand.

intangible—adj. not touchable.

WhizWords

All of 'em.

All-Purpose Words
Celebrity Hot Tub

You can also do this with flash cards—write the word on one side, and the question using the word's definition on the other.

Did you ever want to be one of those reporters on *Entertainment Tonight* or *Access Hollywood* that just spends all of his or her time running around, interviewing celebrities at parties? Or better yet, a VJ on MTV who just hangs out and chats with bands and singers who come by the show's studios? Well, I have.

My idea is that I'd have the celebrities over to my house and interview them sitting in my parents' hot tub. We'd relax in our bathing suits, sip lemonade, and talk about whatever they wanted to talk about. I'm actually thinking about doing this for my public access cable station or doing a webcast. I just haven't figured out how to arrange the microphones without all of us getting electrocuted.

CELEBRITY HOT TUB EXERCISE

For this exercise you are going to need a pad and pencil. Write down "Celebrity Hot Tub" at the top of a page. Now, go to one of the chapters and write down ten words that you are having trouble with. Just read through the words and definitions from one chapter and pick out ten words where you are still a little shaky. Here are ten I picked from Social Studies:

compensation	pragmatist
deter	provoke
eligible	resolute
impose	subversive
insurgent	usurp

Now form a question that you would ask a celebrity who joined you for Celebrity Hot Tub. Use the definition as part of your question. For example, this is a question that I would ask supermodel/actress James King.

Q: Ms. King, are you a pragmatist about your acting career? By that I mean, are you realistic about the roles you are going to get?

After you have written questions using ten words from one chapter, go ahead and write questions with words from the other chapters, too. Keep these all in one place so you can go back and review them (or ask them, should you ever find James King sharing your hot tub).

All-Purpose Words
Word of the Day

You know those daily calendars that look like a block of Post-it Notes? You peel off a page every day and learn something new—every day. My favorite one is the *Far Side* cartoon-of-the-day calendar. I even have a bunch of my favorite *Far Side* calendar pages taped to the inside of my locker. My favorite one is "The Night of the Crash Test Dummies"— it has all these crash test dummies attacking some poor guy in his car.

Anyway, the cool thing about that calendar and all the others is that you get to see something new every day. And that's the best way to learn vocabulary words, by using them every day.

Related Word
consecutive—**adj. occurring in order, one right after the other. For this exercise, you are going to be learning words consecutively, one right after the other.**

VOCABULARY CALENDAR EXERCISE
Until I can convince my book's publisher to make a WordWhiz word-a-day calendar, you are going to have to make one for yourself! This exercise will take an afternoon, so wait until you have a few hours to kill—maybe when it's raining out or you are home sick from school—to get started.

You can make this calendar one of two ways:

> With a brick of Post-It Notes
> With some other "something-a-day" calendar

If you use Post-Its, first go through them and make them into a calendar, writing down the days and months left in this year. (Use a wall calendar to find the correct days.)

If you use another calendar, find one that has a lot of blank space where you can write down a word and its definition.

Now, there are over 600 words in this book. You need to choose the 365 words (or however many days are left on your calendar) that you need to learn the most. Now write the word and its definition on your calendar.

When you are done, put your calendar somewhere you will see it the first thing in the morning: by your bed, on the sink in the bathroom—wherever. Read the word-a-day aloud, repeat it and its definition three times, then put it in your pocket. Try to use that word as much as you can on its day.

Word Whiz

Florida Middle School

Answer Pages

Here are my answers to the Whiz Quizzes and Exercises.
To find out how you did on quizzes and exercises that ask you
to write essays, create calendars, and otherwise use
your creativity, run your answer past an adult who can decide whether
you have used the vocabulary words correctly.

Language Arts

Whiz Quizzes

page 8
Use an adjective or adverb to
describe each of these words:

I go to a *small* school.

My mom had a *fabulous* shopping
experience last week—she got four
pairs of shoes for the price of one.

Difficult tests make me
concentrate even harder.

My soccer team has *bright*
green uniforms.

I play a lot of *physical* sports, like
soccer and football.

The pizza at lunch today was
unbelievably chewy. It was like
eating pizza-flavored gum.

page 13
Write the following sentences
using metaphors:

Pam is <u>greased lightning</u>.

James is <u>two French fries short of a
Happy Meal</u>.

Fabio <u>vacuums up ice cream</u>
like there is no tomorrow.

page 14
Write down your favorite (or least
favorite) platitude:

Least favorite: Life is a bowl of cherries.

page 14
Write down the premise of the
last movie you saw:

There's Something About Mary
Everyone was in love with a girl
named Mary, but only one geeky guy
was her soulmate.

page 15
Write a one-sentence summary
of the last book you read:

The Old Man and the Sea
An old man hadn't caught any fish in
quite some time, then he caught the
biggest fish anyone had ever seen and had
to bring it in to shore all by himself.

Social Studies

Whiz Quizzes
page 20
Name three rules at school that
you advocate:

1. You must raise your hand before
   answering a question.

2. Maintaining a 3.0 GPA gets
   you in unsupervised study hall.

3. No shirt, no shoes, no service.

page 21
Write down your three most
arduous classes in school:

Math
Science
Social Studies

page 29
List three things you once
thought were futile:

1. Getting Grant Hill to
   play for the Orlando Magic.

2. Reaching a height of 5 feet tall.

3. Achieving the high score on
   Arctic Thunder.

page 30
Who was the first president to
be impeached?

President Andrew Johnson

page 34
Name your nemesis!

Murray Freeman, the top junior golfer in
our region. Whenever he beats me, he
rubs it in by asking, "Who taught you to
swing like that? A monkey?" That really
burns me.

Name your favorite team's
main opposition:

The Atlanta Braves

page 37
List three regulations at your school:

1. No chewing gum in class.
2. For boys, no T-shirts: all
shirts must have collars.
3. For girls, no skirts: only
dresses and slacks.

page 39
Name a limitation you have
had to transcend in your life:

I was really impatient a few years
ago and got upset over unimportant
things. I have worked hard to
be more patient and mellow.

Exercises
page 41
Government

Country	Year	Government
England	1714	Monarchy
Texas	1836	Republic
United States	1897	Democracy
Germany	1935	Fascism
Jordan	1953	Monarchy
Cambodia	1976	Despotism
England	1979	Democracy

Math

Whiz Quizzes

page 47

Pick the next number in these number patterns:

3, 6, 9, 12, <u>15</u>

−3, −1, 1, 3, <u>5</u>

3/4, 1 1/2, 2 1/4, <u>3</u>

page 48

Circle the integers.

1/2

.6

(6)

(−6)

(−2)

(0)

3.2

6.9

3/4

(17)

(−12)

(243)

page 52

Solve the following problems with the variables $x=2$ and $y=3$:

$2x = 2(2) = 4$

$4y = 4(3) = 12$

$−5y = −5(3) = −15$

$x − y = 2 − 3 = −1$

$2y + 7x = 2(3) + 7(2) = 6 + 14 = 20$

$−2x − 4y = −2(2) − 4(3) = −4 − 12 = −16$

Exercises

Circles

page 55

Quarter	d= 2(1in) = 2 in
	c= 2π(1in) =2π in
CD	d= 2(7 cm) = 14 cm
	c= 2π(7 cm) = 14π cm
Tire	d= 2(12 in) = 24 in
	c= 2π(12 in) = 24π in

Number Types

page 56

$.79$

positive number, rational number

$.327$

positive number, rational number

2 1/2

positive number, prime number, rational number

4

integer, positive number, rational number

-12

integer, negative number, rational number

6π

irrational number, positive number

Number Relationships

page 57

	Mean	Median	Mode
English	85.71	92	92
Math	85.43	82	78
Science	94.43	94	94
Social Studies	83.86	84	84
O'Neill	.291	.285	.256
Ramirez	.313	.309	none
Rodriguez	.300	.305	none
Jeter	.323	.324	none
Gwynn	.336	.329	.317

Science

Whiz Quizzes

page 62
Name three organisms that are part of an ecosystem at or near your home.

1. Koi fish
2. cat
3. front lawn

Name three more extinct animals or species.

1. Dodo bird
2. Tasmanian tiger wolf
3. Sea cow

page 63
Think of a name for your generation that is better than Generation I.

My pick: Generation Perfect

page 64
Identify the rock's type:

Basalt—igneous
Granite—igneous
Limestone—sedimentary
Marble—metamorphic

page 65
What's another kind of insulation?

My sleeping bag insulates me from the cold when I camp out.

List three things that are lethal to humans:

1. Some kinds of cancer
2. Power lines
3. Extreme hot or cold

page 67
Name a genetic mutation that helped this species survive:
Giraffe—long neck
Human—opposable thumbs
Elephant—big tusks
Cheetah—extreme speed

page 71
What kinds of sustainable crops are produced in your part of the state?

Grapefruit and oranges.

Nature is full of transformations. Name three:

1. Caterpillars transform into butterflies.
2. Ice transforms into water (and vice versa).
3. Seeds transform into flowers.

Answer Pages

Exercises
The Body
page 73–75

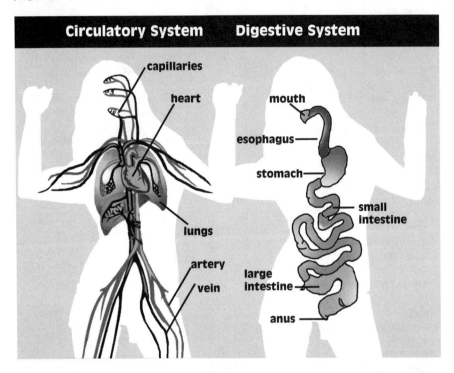

Circulatory System
capillaries
heart
lungs
artery
vein

Digestive System
mouth
esophagus
stomach
small intestine
large intestine
anus

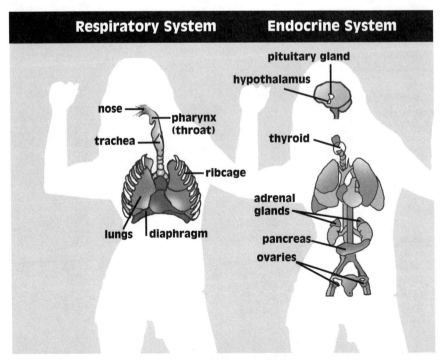

Respiratory System
nose
pharynx (throat)
trachea
ribcage
lungs
diaphragm

Endocrine System
pituitary gland
hypothalamus
thyroid
adrenal glands
pancreas
ovaries

Test Instructions

Whiz Quizzes

page 80

Circle your answers to the following "best" questions:

Man
Better
Right

page 82

Circle the facts and underline the opinions.

The Marlins won the World Series in 1997.

They are going to win it again this year.

The Marlins beat the Braves for the NL pennant in 1997.

The Marlins will beat the Braves every time they meet next year.

Charles Johnson is the best catcher in the Major Leagues.

All-Purpose Words

Whiz Quizzes

page 86

List the three classmates you collaborate with most:

Frank
Judy
Mookie

Also Available

20-Minute Learning Connection:
Florida Middle School Edition

Crusade in the Classroom:
How George W. Bush's Education Reforms
Will Affect Your Children, Our Schools

No-Stress Guide to the 8th Grade FCAT,
Second Edition